THE
CONNECTOR'S COMPASS

NAVIGATE YOUR WAY TO
MEANINGFUL RELATIONSHIPS

JOE KOUFMAN

Published by Ripples Media
Atlanta, GA
www.ripples.media

First printing 2026

Cover design by Joe Koufman & Ripples Media
Book interior by Najdan Mancic

ISBN 979-8-9936722-1-2 Paperback
ISBN 979-8-9936722-2-9 Hardback
ISBN 979-8-9936722-0-5 eBook

Library of Congress Control Number: On File

For Joss and Radley—my true north. May your circle stay wide, your roots run deep, and your doors open for others. May your compass always point to kindness, curiosity, and courage, and may you find your people and be theirs.

TABLE OF CONTENTS

FOREWORD

I t was the fall of 1992. A group of earnest, volunteer-minded Wake Forest University students had gathered to plan the annual Project Pumpkin event. Our goal was audacious: bring children from across Winston-Salem onto the campus for trick-or-treating throughout the university and a giant carnival on the main lawn. It promised great fun for everyone, but it was no minor endeavor. Our small team was charged with inviting hundreds of children (and convincing their caregivers it was safe) and with persuading other university students and faculty to dress up, hand out candy, and staff the carnival. Not only that, but we also had to recruit sponsors ranging from local mom-and-pop companies to multinational enterprises to donate candy and supplies.

For Project Pumpkin to succeed, everyone in the network had to understand the big goal, embrace their role in it, and share our excitement—not just on the day of the event, but leading up to it and afterwards so it would endure year after year. (It has.)

I was new to Wake, so I had only begun to build friendships. I was choosing my first friends carefully, making sure they were the kind of people I could work, play, and live around for the coming years. So, I didn't yet know the exuberant, charismatic junior who was buzzing through the gathering of students. He was stoking excitement, communicating details, and creating connections.

Spoiler. That was early-days Joe Koufman. Better than most other group leaders, Joe already knew how to communicate the pieces of a project vision and plan. Unlike almost anyone else, Joe also knew how to connect people to the project vision and plan—and to each other. If this were a nature and nurture study, Joe would have been the rare example of someone who showcased both.

In the decades since meeting one of the most naturally gifted connectors to walk the planet, Joe and I have had the opportunity to become friends, collaborators, and colleagues many times over.

The list includes Project Pumpkin. Many years later, he would connect me to another tremendously impactful nonprofit called 48in48. He's played a role in helping to introduce friends, colleagues, mentees, and philanthropic collaborators. In the early days of launching my brand agency Watchword, Joe connected me to Kelly Deen, then the VP of Marketing for the unicorn startup Magic Leap. He knew she needed a contract partner with a market intelligence, brand, and content background—and that we would work well together. We did. The project was a success, and I was positioned to grow Watchword fivefold.

Again, Joe's vision for the connection went far beyond the project's needs. He recognized that the Magic Leap and Watchword *people* were a good match.

Later in this book, Joe shares another story of a "Setup" that dramatically contributed to advancing Watchword's trajectory. Keep reading until you find the story. His vision and actions are an impressive master class in spotting opportunities and connecting the right people to bring them to life. As you read your way through the book to find the story, you'll benefit from Joe's experience and valuable guidance.

Here's the thing about great connectors and networkers: they may not be the most detailed, the most disciplined, the most highly educated, or even the most visionary person in the room. But they are the one who understands the needs of organizations, projects, and individuals in ways that others do not. They tend to listen, hear, and remember details in ways that others do not. They participate in networking events and dedicate time to connecting in ways that others do not. And, perhaps most importantly, they *care* about widening networks and deepening relationships between people in ways that others do not.

Joe is among the greatest connectors and networkers of them all. The proof is in this book.

I've known Joe for more than 30 years. I thought I'd witnessed (and benefitted from) the skills that have put him at the front and center of the many efforts we have shared over the years. But the pages of this book contain even more depth and knowledge.

In *The Connector's Compass*, Joe does what he does best. He uses his skills and resources to meet the needs of others—you. Read every page with a highlighter in hand. Dog-ear the ones that speak to you most. Even if connecting isn't natural to you, this book will help you nurture new ways of using curiosity to connect the dots, develop more productive listening skills, and build the confidence to show up with authority.

I have learned a lot from Joe over the years, but the greatest lesson is this: people want to be connected. We know that purposeful relationships can transform lives. Still, most of us aren't naturally great at taking the initiative or building the courage to make the introduction. Joe is great at it. In this book, he helps you nurture those skills so you can be too.

Rachelle Kuramoto,

Brand & Content Strategy Executive

PROLOGUE

Many of my friends and family members have asked me why I chose to write this book. The short answer is that I initially thought that everyone's brain worked the same way mine does.

I am naturally curious about people—when I ask them questions, I am genuinely interested in their responses. I file away seemingly trivial bits of information to be dug out from my memory during a key opportunity to connect with them again, or with another person.

My brain works like a crime-scene corkboard, with red thread connecting the suspects, victims, and other seemingly disparate nodes. I am able to summon (seemingly purposeless) trivia about people at just the right time to make a connection between two presumably disjointed individuals. Some have said that this skill is a gift, but I believe it is very learnable. Once I discovered that not everyone thinks the way I do, I felt compelled to write this book and to enable others to build skills for making meaningful connections.

This book is entitled the *Connector's Compass* because, ironically, as a person who has been described as "directionally challenged," I have always been fascinated by compasses.

When I was a kid, I took an orienteering "class" in summer camp where we learned to use compasses to navigate in the woods. The idea of a small gadget that assists us in finding our way as we move through the world has always appealed to me.

I hope that this book can be your guide. I want to be your sherpa, helping you navigate as you form and nurture relationships that can benefit others and eventually you. I am excited for you to join me on this journey.

INTRODUCTION

I love connecting people. In fact, three couples eventually married after I made initial introductions for them.

I made my first successful match in college, the second was as a newly minted couple of college graduates, and the third was two young professionals. All three couples ended up having successful marriages that each produced two children. The best part about being a matchmaker is seeing the joy that others receive from being connected. I always find it rewarding to connect people from completely different aspects of my life.

Apparently, I am one of the rare people who have been able to convert my lifelong passion into my profession. In 2014, this zeal for matchmaking drove me to start a company, Setup, focused on unlocking the power of human connection by matching brands and marketing agencies together. In the first ten years of the business, we made over 1,200 introductions between client-side and agency-side marketers. We've worked with incredible brands like The Coca-Cola Company, Brooks Running, Great Clips, Boys & Girls Clubs of America, and NCR, connecting them with innovative marketing agencies that would help them solve problems and reach new customers.

The brands and marketing organizations we connected have generated value and revenue from these partnerships. On a more human level, each time we meet with a client to outline their marketing challenges and then leverage those insights to pair them with qualified marketing agencies, it gives me and my team a spark of joy.

That joy of making meaningful connections, both personally and professionally, led me to write this book.

During over 30 years of matchmaking, I have learned that the skills that formed the foundation of my business are not intrinsic, they can be developed and fine-tuned. In writing this book, I aim to provide a guidebook for those who, unlike me, are not natural matchmakers but want to learn these skills.

I have a friend who is a natural introvert. He loves reading and needs to recharge after social events. Years ago, he was building a company and realized that these skills were crucial for the company's growth. By practicing the skills I now outlined in this book, he has transformed himself into one of the best connectors I have ever met. He is a skilled orator, an influential connector of people, and comfortable in any social situation.

While you may not be building a company, you have life goals that cannot be achieved alone. There is an often-circulated proverb that says: "If you want to go fast, go alone; but if you want to go far, go together." The need to connect with others is inherent to us as humans (it has been since the days of cavemen), and you will need the support of others to reach your objectives.

Your career depends on becoming good at these skills. Think about the last time you were hired or hired someone. The person you were interviewing was likely sitting in that seat because of a relationship or connection.

Simply put, it is rare for companies to hire individuals with whom they have no prior connection. All companies want to minimize risk. When it comes to hiring, that usually means selecting a candidate who is a known quantity, or at least someone who has been recommended.

Marissa King is a professor of Organizational Behavior at the Yale School of Management. In her book *Social Chemistry*, King introduces the idea that there are three basic types of networkers:

1. **Expansionists**

2. **Brokers**

3. **Conveners**

She writes that "expansionists have extraordinarily large networks, brokers bring together typically disconnected parties from different worlds, and conveners build dense networks in which their friends are also friends."[1]

In other words, expansionists want to build as big a network as possible, brokers want to bring diverse connections together, and conveners build deep, and often (smaller) interconnected, networks. In practice: expansionists grow breadth, brokers bridge groups, conveners deepen tight circles."

The purpose of King's framework is to better leverage the style that's most comfortable to you, and then develop the skills that may not come as naturally. It may also be helpful to shift between styles depending on the situation. For instance, you might

---

[1] King, Marissa, *Social Chemistry*. (New York: Penguin Random House, 2020).

be an expansionist when you're building your business (and growing your client base), or a convener when you're nurturing the business (building engagement and retention for your existing team).

Of course, most individuals do not fit into one specific type of network *all of the time.* Skilled connectors leverage different styles for different seasons. King's framework is helpful as we examine how to build connections not only for professional advancement, but for personal growth. If we are in touch with our own personality, as well as how we want to best leverage our networks based on where we are professionally, "networking" feels far less arduous and overwhelming.

In addition to professional advantage, honing these skills leads to fulfillment and prosperity. The end goal is *not* to seek the benefits. Personal gratification comes from making and nurturing connections.

The good news is that one does not have to be a naturally born super-connector to benefit from honing these matchmaking skills. They can be learned by following the advice in this book, and it will pay dividends of fulfillment and social currency to improve your relationships and your career.

On a primal level, we all crave human connections with each other, yet many of us struggle to form new relationships and nurture them, especially as adults.

There is a common expression, "your network is your net worth," but many people consider networking a dirty word. It is inherently transactional—meeting purely for the sake of furthering your own professional interests. The idea of attending a "networking event" can elicit fear and anxiety from even the most extroverted professionals. Standing in a crowded room making small talk with people you've never met, usually solely for a business function, ranks right up there with a root canal as a joyful experience.

Networking doesn't have to feel like pulling teeth. With the right mindset, you can master these skills, even if they do not come naturally. Some of the attributes that are crucial for making good connections include curiosity, warmth, creativity, and authenticity. Rather than trying to become the "networking guru" who hands out business cards to anyone who will take them, focus on making ONE great connection.

These skills can be demonstrated in person, but they can also be exhibited through email, Slack, social media, phone, and other channels. The same principles that apply to in-person events are crucial for digital communications. Digital channels can reinforce relationships and also provide a bridge connecting people across geographies.

By leveraging the skills in this book and putting them into practice, you will become empowered to create deeper relationships that will open up new opportunities for others and support your professional growth. Putting these skills into action—helping others connect with people who will benefit them—will serve as a guide, a compass if you will, to short-term joy and long-term fulfillment.

Here's what I need you to understand: these skills don't come naturally to most people, and they certainly don't develop overnight. I have worked hard to develop in the areas where I am weak.

Let me tell you a story about learning something new.

After the pandemic gripped the world in early 2020, my uncle remembered my (unfulfilled) interest in the trumpet fueled during my post-college years living in New Orleans. He had found my grandmother's high school marching band trumpet in his basement and offered to ship it to me. When I received it, I marveled that this exact horn had been played 75 years earlier by my very own grandmother. I decided to rekindle my passion and sought out the best trumpet player in the Southeast, Joe Gransden, to teach me to play it. We began lessons via video for many months until we felt safe enough to meet in person.

While I have picked up and put down that trumpet many times over the years since, I have learned a lot about the amount of work it requires to master new skills. **It takes courage to "suck" at something new.**

Just like learning to play a new instrument, making connections requires practice. My wish is that you will find the fortitude to practice the skills I outline in this book. As Rachelle Kuramoto wrote in the foreword, I hope you will dog-ear and highlight the pages of this book as you practice the skills that will propel your career and life. Each time you put in the work to make new connections for others and yourself, you "flex that muscle" and make it easier the next time. While some of the concepts outlined in this book may scare you, you may also find that with some practice, they will bring you joy.

DEMONSTRATING
CURIOSITY

In any human interaction, curiosity weaves a vibrant pattern of connections and serves as the catalyst to transform strangers into acquaintances, and acquaintances into friends. In my opinion, people who are inquisitive are more intelligent than people who are not. It is fun to learn what "makes people tick." Hearing the backstories that lead to the current state of the world enriches our lives and creates cues that could prove useful down the line. I have tried to surround myself with people who are curious about others and the world, and I strive to remain constantly curious.

Curiosity is fostered through three basic tenets, including active listening, maintaining eye contact, and asking great questions.

THE ART OF ACTIVE LISTENING

When one enters a room, the goal is not merely to be seen or heard, but to see and listen to others, as well as understand their stories, challenges, and aspirations—this is the essence of active listening.

It is an engaging, dynamic process. It's about fully concentrating on the person speaking, understanding their message, responding thoughtfully, and remembering the conversation.

When I meet with clients at Setup, I practice active listening with each coffee meeting, video call, or networking event. I ask questions about the person's life, not just their business. Where did they grow up? Tell me about their siblings. What kind of music do they love? What are their favorite hobbies? **The goal is to understand the person.** There is plenty of time to learn more about their business life. Some of my former clients have become some of my best friends, largely due to my demonstrated genuine interest in them and their families.

To hone this skill, practice the following:

■ **Be Present:** In a world brimming with distractions, offering your undivided attention is a rare gift. Resist the urge to check your phone or think about your next meeting. Instead, focus on the person in front of you. Your attentiveness will help you grasp the nuances of the conversation and convey respect and appreciation.

■ **Encourage Sharing:** Use open-ended questions that prompt thought-provoking responses. Instead of asking, "Did you enjoy the event?" try, "What about your hobby intrigues you most?" Instead of asking "What was your first concert?" try, "What was a concert that moved you?" In both cases, the second question elicits a deeper response that encourages further exploration. Questions like these demonstrate your interest and encourage a more detailed and meaningful exchange.

- **Reflect and Clarify:** Occasionally paraphrase the speaker's words and reflect them back to them. This shows that you are actively engaged and ensures you have correctly understood their message. If you have any confusion, ask for clarification.

- **Notice Non-Verbal Cues:** So much of communication is non-verbal. Nodding your head, maintaining eye contact, and leaning in slightly are all signs of active engagement—whether in-person or on a video call. These cues silently communicate your interest and encourage the speaker to continue.

Techniques for Sparking Meaningful Conversations

While small talk is a common starting point, deeper, more meaningful conversations truly connect people. Here are techniques to elevate your conversations from mundane to memorable:

- **Find Common Ground:** Begin with broad topics and focus on shared interests or experiences. Discovering a shared passion for a hobby, profession, or cause can quickly transform a polite conversation into a vibrant exchange.

■ **Share Stories, Not Just Facts:** As former poet laureate and Wake Forest professor, Maya Angelou famously said: "I've learned that people will forget what you said, people will forget what you did, but people will never forget how you made them feel." Sharing personal stories or insights allows for emotional connections, making the conversation more memorable.

■ **Be Genuinely Enthusiastic:** Enthusiasm is palpable and contagious. People can easily tell when you are excited to learn more about them, and it encourages the other person to open up and share more freely. A light smile is never a bad way to demonstrate enthusiasm to someone with whom you are engaging.

■ **Practice Empathy:** Try to see the world from the other person's perspective. Empathy builds trust and understanding, key components of any meaningful relationship.

THE IMPORTANCE OF EYE CONTACT

Jennifer Dorian is the President and CEO of WABE, Atlanta's NPR radio and TV station. Before that, she was a senior leader with Turner Broadcasting Systems (now Warner Bros. Discovery) and The Coca-Cola Company. Jennifer has succeeded in the notoriously competitive media landscape by genuinely connecting with people.

One key reason Jennifer has flourished in her business career is her demonstrated high EI (Emotional Intelligence). When you interact with Jennifer, she makes you feel like you are the only person on the planet. This rare skill makes her the right person to provide tips on how to demonstrate curiosity about people.

She said that while it sounds simplistic, eye contact is one of the most important steps to establishing connections. "It's important to look at people (as you are walking down a hallway, for example, and say hello) and actually see them—read their mood, and be available to interact. Eye contact is the invitation to connect."

Eye contact conveys being present. In an age of smartphones and endless distractions, this can seem like a lost art, but it has a profound impact on the people you are around.

"Holding eye contact while people speak to you is very important," she said. "Is there anything worse than someone looking down at their phone while you're trying to talk to them? Or a person at a party looking around the room or over your shoulder while you're trying to connect with them? So, of course, helping people feel seen starts with looking at them."

As the old adage goes, "The eyes are the window to the soul." Making direct eye contact with another person demonstrates that you are taking the time and care to see them. In order to make real connections with others, they must feel as if you care about them. Persistent and direct eye contact helps the other person know that you see them literally and figuratively.

Beyond eye contact, Jennifer emphasizes the power of complementary body language.

Smile gently as you enter a conversation—not a forced grin, but a natural expression of openness. Keep your body language inviting by avoiding crossed arms, and subtly mirror the other person's tone and tempo. These nonverbal cues work together to build subconscious rapport and signal that you're fully present.

I could not agree more with Jennifer's perspective: "It's vital to ask questions, listen, take turns speaking, ask follow-up questions, and spend a little time! Finding common ground, shared passions, and new perspectives is a lot of fun—but takes more than three minutes.

"If I'm in a group setting, I'm far more likely to spend most of my time getting to know three or four people pretty well versus working the whole room. I find working a room exhausting, but meeting three or four new people is energizing and rewarding."

For me, asking great questions that demonstrate your interest is key. Rather than surface-level "what" questions, asking "why or how" questions gets to the core emotion behind decisions. These deeper inquiries help you build trust and empathy in a way that more straightforward conversations do not.

The format of the questions should not be accusatory, like "Why would you have done something like that?" but instead, should be asked from a place of empathy.

A good example of a question that demonstrates curiosity and empathy, is, "How did you feel when you had to make that incredibly painful choice?" This approach invites vulnerability and gets to the emotional core of someone's experience, creating space for authentic connection to flourish.

ASKING QUESTIONS TO NURTURE RELATIONSHIPS

Demonstrating curiosity extends beyond nonverbal communication. Abby England, the Head of Marketing for Elevate Structures, also emphasizes that curiosity not only pays off in the moment at events, but also has a much longer-term effect.

"The best way to nurture relationships?" she shares. "Be genuinely curious. Ask real questions. **Listen—like really listen—and remember the details.**"

Being able to recall those facts about individuals presents opportunities to connect later. Recollecting those moments of conversation days or months later can have a real impact.

Why is this? Everyone appreciates being listened to and feeling as if they made an impact on someone. Being memorable makes people feel interesting and important.

Abby points out that, too often, individuals assume that these points of reconnection need to be emotional or influential. They don't. They simply need to be entry points to pick the conversation (and the relationship) back up.

"When something reminds you of that person, reach out," she said. "It doesn't have to be formal or heavy. A simple, 'Saw this and thought of you' text can go a long way. I try to offer something useful—a connection, a podcast recommendation, a genuine compliment—without expecting something in return. It makes follow-ups easier because it's grounded in mutual respect, not obligation."

> **Again, the most important point is that it only feels artificial if the conversation or question isn't genuine.**

People generally have a good sense of when a connection is actually curious about their career path, favorite restaurant spot, or most embarrassing story, or when they're simply nodding their head and barely paying attention. If you are interested in the relationship only transactionally, people will sense it. If you come across as genuine, the other person will likely receive it that way. As Dale Carnegie famously said: "To be interesting, be interested."

Here are some of Abby's tips for asking questions earnestly.

- Be curious, not performative.

- Don't be afraid to follow up, people love to be thought of.

- Use informal, familiar language. Make it feel easy and genuine.

- Let go of the idea that it's "weird" to reconnect after time has passed. If someone comes to mind, there's probably a reason.

Asking great questions makes people feel "seen" and leads to deeper connections.

IMPROVING IN-PERSON INTERACTIONS

Beyond asking thoughtful questions and remembering details, here are some other practical tips for making in-person interactions seem more genuine. As you continue to practice these, they will come more naturally.

"Name, Anchor, Ask"

First, I use the "Name, Anchor, Ask" framework. It's a simple formula meant to get the conversation started and keep the energy moving.

- **Name:** Say their name early and often. "Hi John, it's nice to meet you."

- **Anchor:** Find a shared context or compliment. "I loved what you said in the session earlier," or "I have been so impressed with how interesting the people are at this event!"

- **Ask:** Follow with a light question: "What brought you here today?" or "What's something you're hoping to get out of today's event?"

You'll find that these three steps work in any number of professional settings.Some leaders especially dread bigger group events (and would rather spend two hours at the DMV than at a mixer event). As a result, having this simple construct in your toolbox can reduce anxiety if you're not a natural extrovert.

Be the Host

Another tip is to adopt a "host's mindset," even if you're a guest. Here are some ideas for succeeding as a host, even when it's not your party!

- Welcome people who are entering the party and give them a verbal tour. For example: "Your coat goes here, the drinks and food are there, the restroom is down the hall."

- Introduce people to each other. ("Hey, you both work in marketing for nonprofits! You should meet!")

- Offer help. ("Can I grab you a water?" or "Let's go find your seat together.")

- Be attuned to anyone standing alone or who appears disengaged and engage them.

When you're the host at any event, you want people to have a good time and feel comfortable. This approach is all about internalizing this mindset in whatever room you're in.

> **When you adopt this mindset, you shift your focus from "How am I doing?" to "How can I make others feel more comfortable?"**

Welcoming people and making them feel valued helps them feel connected to you as the "host," and leaves a positive impression for putting them at ease.

Small Talk That Doesn't Feel Small

Leveraging observational comments (for example: "I noticed your notebook has the AIMS logo—were you involved in planning it?") is another way to foster connection during in-person interactions.

Sometimes, observational comments get portrayed as painful and awkward (think of the "We can't help you from becoming your parents" in the spot-on Progressive commercials). However, inane chatter, like "We sure did need the rain" or "The traffic getting here was terrible," isn't what we're talking about here. **If your comments and observations come across as mundane and boring, so will you.**

However, if you demonstrate curiosity and ask thoughtful questions, learning useful tidbits about the person with whom you're having a discussion, the conversation will come far easier than you think. In short, if you struggle to find something to say, use what's in your environment (in person or on a video call) as a natural conversation bridge.

- "I noticed your [shirt/pin/tattoo]. Please tell me more about that."

- "That is an interesting piece of art behind you. What is the story there?"

- "That speaker had a unique perspective on leadership. What do you think?"

- "I always feel awkward at events like this. How do you like to break the ice?"

Observation-based openers feel spontaneous and personalized. Plus, they lower the pressure.

Keep a Few "Lifelines" in your Pocket

Inevitably, the flow of conversation hits a pause. However, you don't have to panic in an awkward silence! There are always a handful of low-stakes questions that you can keep in your back pocket when you need them.

They can be used at any time, but they should be used to prompt an authentic (two way) conversation.

- "What's a project you're excited about right now?"
- "What's a passion of yours outside of work?"
- "How did you get into what you're doing?"
- "What's been your favorite connection at this event so far?"
- "Any books or podcasts you're into lately?"

Questions like these help you steer clear of small talk and into small moments that matter.

Graceful Exits

Along with fostering meaningful conversation, part of the key is also ending it well. It doesn't have to end with a conversation that dries up, followed by an awkward pause, and then gingerly retreating like a soldier escaping enemy lines.

Start with finding a way to connect and keep in touch after the interaction. That lends itself to a clear ending to the conversation, and always gives you the opportunity to follow up later.

Try phrases like "I've really enjoyed talking, I am looking forward to connecting with you again the next time we meet," or "I promised myself I'd meet three new people before I leave. Can we trade info?"

Then, send a quick follow-up note the next day with a reference to something they said. It reinforces the connection and makes you stand out.

Remember that the new connection should not feel (or be) transactional. It is important to be sincere while making an exit from a conversation.

DEMONSTRATING CURIOSITY IN VIRTUAL SETTINGS

These concepts also apply to online interactions. In fact, in the age of Zoom, Google Meet, and Microsoft Teams, a majority of our conversations actually happen over a screen. As a result, establishing rapport and demonstrating curiosity matter just as much on virtual calls, too.

When you are on video calls, it is essential to utilize the tools that simulate the in-person experience of looking a person directly in the eyes. Because you do not receive the additional non-verbal cues you might get when sharing physical space with the other person, it is even more important to utilize direct eye contact.

Is fostering connection on video calls more difficult than in person? Absolutely.

The point here, though, is that if you can master this skill, it will give you a leg up and make you more memorable compared to everyone else, precisely because it is harder.

My friend Tim Hernquist, who is Head of Enterprise Marketing for Jabra, a large audio and video conferencing equipment company, often discusses the importance of audio and video fidelity in making meaningful connections with others during video conferences—which, of course, have become ubiquitous in a post-pandemic world.

To maximize interpersonal connection, it is crucial to optimize your audio/video environment. A quality webcam, earbuds, headset, and microphone are table stakes to improve the fidelity of the connection. Strong WiFi and good front lighting ensure that you don't appear too dark or pixelated.

One trick I've used to simulate direct eye contact is to minimize the size of video windows near the camera, so that you look directly at the person's eyes rather than at a point below the camera. Utilizing hand gestures intentionally can also make your conversation partner feel more at ease.

It is essential to keep your background less distracting by properly setting up your lighting, sound, and hand gestures. This can be achieved simply by staging a few key objects behind you that are significant to you and your potential audience. I have carefully curated items on simple bookshelves behind my office desk with objects that are meaningful to me, such as awards I have won, photos of my family, and a few knick-knacks, including a custom bobble-head doll that was gifted to me, as well as some Atlanta and Georgia memorabilia. These items can serve as nice icebreakers for conversation with new contacts.

When I am not in my office, for video meetings, I have uploaded a photo of those shelves from where my laptop usually is perched. So when I am away, I still have a nice, professional background. I have found that many people are unaware that I am not in my office when I am using that background.

HOW CURIOSITY LEADS TO DEEPER CONNECTIONS

When you're genuinely curious about people, you're not just collecting information; you're showing that you value them as individuals.

This recognition fosters trust and openness, paving the way for more meaningful relationships.

■ **Creates Mutual Respect:** Showing genuine interest in someone else's experiences and perspectives demonstrates respect. This mutual respect forms the foundation of a strong, lasting connection.

■ **Unearths Hidden Synergies:** Through curiosity, you may discover unexpected commonalities or complementary skills and interests, which can lead to exciting collaborations or partnerships.

It is essential to note that sharing common interests should not devolve into "one-upmanship," but instead should demonstrate a shared experience. Listening with an empathetic perspective and acknowledging the experience of the other person goes much further than suggesting a similar shared experience. For example, if someone tells you about an epic concert they attended, rather than sharing your own epic concert story, validate that fantastic experience by asking follow-up questions about it.

The values of validating another person's story are:

- **Fosters Continuous Learning:** Each person you meet has a unique story and perspective. By remaining curious, you turn every interaction into an opportunity to learn and grow.

- **Builds Social Capital:** Your network's strength isn't just in its numbers but in the quality and depth of its relationships. Curiosity deepens these relationships, turning your network into a rich resource for knowledge, opportunities, and support.

On this journey to becoming a better connector, remember that curiosity is not just a tactic; it's a mindset. It's about embracing the joy of discovering new stories, ideas, and possibilities. By demonstrating genuine curiosity about people, you not only enrich your professional network but also enrich your life.

> **As you navigate the intricate maze of human connections, let your curiosity be your compass, guiding you to more meaningful and rewarding relationships.**

As an exercise, consider building a toolbox of great questions that you have readily available to elicit a better conversation and deeper connections. Some great questions in my toolbox include:

- What is a recent experience that had a significant impact on you?

- What is a change you want to see in the world?

- What is the biggest challenge you have overcome?

- What's something you've always wanted to learn to do?

- Who has been a major influence on you, and what did you learn from them?

- What's a life lesson you hope to pass on to the next generation?

At first, these questions may seem like you're trying to conduct an interview, so I would not recommend using all of them in a single conversation. However, using one or two of these questions allows you to go deeper than the typical surface talk. Asking more consequential questions is the point. It demonstrates authentic curiosity.

2

FOSTERING CREATIVITY

C reative people are interesting to others. Creative people are interested in others. I have found that becoming a creative person will benefit you on the journey to building deeper connections with others.

Creativity thrives in the presence of other creative minds. When you align yourself with innovative individuals, their energy, ideas, and perspectives can spark new insights into your thinking. Creativity comes to life in a variety of different ways. Artists, poets, entrepreneurs, musicians, digital creators, writers, and performers synthesize information in their worlds and reconstitute it as new, creative output—such as visual arts, dances, and songs. Engaging with creative people doesn't just expose you to these fresh ideas—it amplifies your ability to generate them yourself. This opens doors to collaborations and opportunities you might not have considered on your own.

> **The magic of creative alignment is that it isn't just about benefiting from others' skills; it's about how their ingenuity fuels your own.**

By surrounding yourself with people who think differently, experiment boldly, and challenge assumptions, you sharpen your ability to connect dots that others may not see. These relationships naturally lead to new ideas for meaningful introductions— bringing together individuals whose combined talents create something greater than the sum of their parts.

I have found that teams that are diverse (in all aspects of that word) are more likely to come up with creative ideas than homogeneous teams. Over the years, I have curated a diverse group at Setup that brings different viewpoints and stimulates curiosity in me and in each other. We have hired young people who make up for their lack of experience with enthusiasm and a fresh perspective. We have hired tenured staff who bring a wealth of experience and skills. We have hired people from different ethnic and socio-economic backgrounds who see the world in a way that differs from my own.

While we do demand that everyone on the team aligns with our company values of Honorable, Approachable, Insightful, Tenacious, and Innovative, there are many people in our world who embody those values but maintain different life perspectives and experiences.

In addition to having a team with diverse perspectives, I aim to foster the curiosity of my team members about the world beyond their work. One fantastic example is Madeline Evans. She was an intern for Setup in 2017, soon after she graduated from the Terry College of Business at the University of Georgia with a BBA degree in Marketing, with an emphasis in Digital Marketing. At the end of her internship, we offered her a job as Marketing Coordinator. While in college, she performed with an improv troupe. Since college, Madeline has grown as a marketer at Setup and a professional improv actor—performing and teaching at various comedy venues throughout Atlanta. Not only do her interests outside of work add value to the creativity she brings to her job, but Madeline also cultivated team-building at Setup through her experience leading improv.

FOSTERING AN ENVIRONMENT OF MUTUAL COLLABORATION

The strongest connections are built through collaboration with creative and skilled individuals. Moira Vetter, the CEO of Modo Modo Agency, points out, though, that cultivating creativity starts with culture, not necessarily the raw talent of the individuals themselves.

"People too often think that creative thinking comes from creative people," said Moira. "In truth, creativity and the energy that sparks innovation come from having a safe space where everyone can think out loud. Napoleon Hill famously referred to this as a 'mastermind principle.' In *Think And Grow Rich,* he asserted that, "No two minds ever come together without, thereby, creating a third, invisible, intangible force which may be likened to a third mind."

Aligning yourself with talented people enhances your capabilities and creates growth opportunities.

By fostering an environment that encourages partnerships with those who excel in creativity and expertise, you open doors to innovation and shared success.

Moira believes that culture will obviously look different for different groups, but the focus should always center on fostering new ideas.

Her framework for fostering creativity? "Set rules and be direct. Learn to be quiet at times and loud at others. Draw pictures on the walls or the floors. Ask people what they mean. And when the eurekas start coming, don't stop! Keep going."

According to Moira, initial ideas tend to be the most obvious ones, the low-hanging fruit that comes easily to mind. The real value emerges when teams push past these surface-level solutions and remain in creative flow long enough to uncover more unique, non-obvious possibilities. This collaborative energy creates something that transcends what any individual could produce working alone. It's the phenomenon Hill described in his concept of the mastermind—a dynamic he compared to a battery with all circuits firing, generating power that exceeds the sum of its individual components.

Having worked with Moira and her team, I can attest that the entire company is dedicated to fostering creativity. Their space is filled with bright, colorful, and collaborative workspaces. Their team can be seen huddling with one another, including an always-on video connection to a key remote employee. I have seen the output of the Modo Modo creative process first-hand when we hired them in 2019 to rebrand my company from AgencySparks to Setup.

My team was blown away by the variety and depth of creative ideas they supplied to us throughout our rebranding process. For example, after Modo Modo conducted an extensive interview process to understand our company and what our priorities were in a new name/brand mark, they came back to us with ten different name options. Once we narrowed them down to the top three, they helped us refine them to select what would become the name Setup. From there, they offered us seven or eight logo treatments—each with wildly different visual elements, so we could pick the top two to refine. It became clear to me and my team that Modo Modo's creative process, and the talent responsible for it, would result in an exciting new brand for us. The enthusiasm from clients and agencies about our new brand validated our decision.

CULTIVATING A CULTURE

Success is rarely a solo endeavor. Recognizing and aligning with the right creative people allows you to expand your skill set and maximize opportunities. Whether you're leading a team, building a network, or seeking fresh ideas, embracing the strengths of those around you fosters an atmosphere of innovation and trust.

Effective collaboration can be fostered through:

- Actively engaging with creative individuals and valuing their input.

- Seeking out diverse perspectives to drive innovative solutions.

- Encouraging an open exchange of ideas and expertise.

- Supporting and amplifying the contributions of others.

When people feel valued for their contributions, they are more likely to invest in the collective success of the group. The more engaged the individuals are, the more likely they are to come up with innovative solutions.

Creative leaders like Moira emphasize that successful creative collaboration requires participants who are genuinely invested in the outcome. "If there is no skin in the game, the quality of the thinking is low. Participants must care. We've all worked with people with amazing skills who don't seem to care. Get them out of the meeting or the discussion. Caring about what happens is a requirement for contributing or voting on the quality of ideas."

The process for fostering new creative ideas could look something like this:

Cultivating a Culture of Respect

- **Encourage Open Communication:** Establish forums where team members can openly share ideas and feedback. Emphasize the importance of active listening and respectful dialogue.

- **Recognize and Reward:** Regularly acknowledge each team member's contributions. Develop a reward system that celebrates both individual and collective achievements.

Building Trust and Team Spirit

- **Team-Building Activities:** Organize events and activities that are not only fun but also enhance teamwork and understanding among members.

- **Transparency in Operations:** Ensure all team members know the company's goals, challenges, and achievements. This transparency fosters a sense of ownership and belonging.

Building Trust and Synergy

Strong partnerships are built on trust. When you align yourself with talented individuals, trust creates the foundation for a successful working relationship. Trust enables you to rely on each other's strengths, delegate effectively, and push creative boundaries without fear of failure. Here are some great ways to carry this out.

- Be consistent in your actions and follow through on commitments.

- Create an environment where feedback is constructive and mutual.

■ Show respect for different working styles and approaches.

■ Emphasize collective wins over individual accolades.

Trust fosters an environment where creative minds can flourish together, leading to stronger connections and more impactful outcomes.

IDENTIFYING AND ALIGNING WITH TALENTED INDIVIDUALS

A key component of building valuable relationships is identifying the right people with whom to collaborate. The most successful individuals actively seek out those whose strengths complement their own.

Recognizing Key Skills and Strengths

Not all valuable skills are immediately obvious. Being intentional about identifying and engaging with people who bring diverse strengths can significantly enhance your capabilities.

While there's a tendency to think that creative individuals are predominantly designers and writers, creative thinking goes well beyond our typical definition of *creative* occupations.

Creative thinking extends far beyond traditional "creative" roles. Some of the most innovative minds can be found among engineers, CFOs, and other business professionals. While entrepreneurs are widely recognized for their creativity, great ideas can come from anywhere in an organization.

Here are some ways to recognize valuable skills in others:

- Observe how individuals naturally approach challenges—do they bring analytical thinking, creative problem-solving, or interpersonal strengths?

- Pay attention to their ability to execute ideas effectively.

- Identify those who are passionate and committed to their craft.

- Engage in conversations that reveal unique insights and expertise.

Aligning yourself with people who have complementary skills will help you navigate complex challenges and unlock new opportunities.

Leveraging Diverse Perspectives

The best collaborations thrive on diversity.

Surrounding yourself with people with different perspectives and expertise leads to richer ideas and more well-rounded strategies.

To effectively leverage diverse perspectives:

- Be intentional about seeking out individuals from different industries and backgrounds.

- Encourage collaboration that combines technical expertise with creative thinking.

- Recognize that innovation often comes from unexpected connections.

- Create spaces where different skillsets can work together toward a shared goal.

By aligning yourself with creative people who bring fresh ideas, you expand your potential and create a network that fosters continuous learning and success.

SURROUND YOURSELF WITH PEOPLE WHO INSPIRE YOU

Success is built on relationships. Aligning with creative and skilled individuals allows you to enhance your expertise, navigate challenges more effectively, and unlock new opportunities. By fostering a culture of collaboration, identifying valuable talent, and embracing diverse perspectives, you set yourself up for long-term success.

Make it a habit to surround yourself with people whose creativity and skills inspire you. Look for opportunities to connect with these people by frequenting places (art galleries, concerts, museums, parks) where creative people gather. Strong connections lead to stronger outcomes, and by engaging with the right individuals, you build a network that drives innovation and meaningful success.

3

LEVERAGING YOUR ADHD

We all have moments, even the most focused among us, where we tend to feel distracted, remarking that "we're feeling a little ADHD today."

In my case, this is actually true. I received an Attention Deficit and Hyperactivity Disorder (ADHD) diagnosis as an adult. Over the years, it has definitely created some challenges, including finding the time to literally sit down and write this book! However, I firmly believe that my professional success, as an entrepreneur, marketer, and connector, would not have been possible were it not for my ADHD. I believe that there is a strong tendency for highly creative people to have ADHD attributes. I also believe there are ways everyone can lean into ADHD tendencies to spark greater creativity and even productivity.

According to the National Survey of Children's Health, over 6 million (9.8%) children have been diagnosed with ADHD. More adults have been diagnosed than in years past. Add this fact to the reality that notifications can take the form of chimes, bells, vibrations, bouncing icons, etc. According to Reviews. org, Americans check their phones 144 times per day, and 75% of Americans check their phones within five minutes of receiving a notification.

We are all distracted, and our attention spans are shorter than ever. Between constant notifications, endless scrolling, and the pressure to multitask, modern life has created ADHD-like conditions for nearly everyone. So it turns out, we are all a little ADHD and can benefit from learning to harness these tendencies.

THE HIDDEN STRENGTHS OF ADHD

While ADHD can be a challenge for those of us who struggle to execute tasks and complete projects, it can be leveraged as a strength if we know how to harness the upside. In social settings, being able to rapidly communicate with multiple people about various topics can be an advantage.

Those with ADHD typically have higher energy levels, are often great storytellers, and tend to be more spontaneous, which can enhance likability in social situations. Also, while those with ADHD can occasionally get sidetracked, jumping from topic to topic, when they are passionate about a topic, it can trigger hyper-focus.

I find that I am able to rapidly connect with new people quickly by thinking on my feet, telling great stories, and leveraging my creativity to help others solve problems they face.

Over my career, here are some of the assets and liabilities of ADHD:

The Unseen Assets

■ **Rapid Information Processing:** Individuals with ADHD often process information rapidly, allowing them to quickly absorb and react to new stimuli. This trait is a tremendous asset in fast-paced environments where adaptability is crucial.

- **Creative Problem-Solving:** The unique neural pathways in the ADHD brain foster out-of-the-box thinking. This leads to innovative solutions and fresh perspectives, invaluable in brainstorming sessions or when tackling complex problems.

- **Hyper-Focus:** While managing multiple tasks can be challenging when a topic truly captivates someone with ADHD, they can enter a state of hyper-focus. This intense concentration allows for deep dives into subjects, leading to expert-level knowledge and insights.

- **High Energy and Enthusiasm:** The natural zest and dynamism of individuals with ADHD can be infectious, making them excellent motivators and leaders. Their energy can uplift teams and drive projects forward.

The Hurdles to Overcome

- **Distraction and Time Management:** The flip side of rapid information processing is the tendency to become easily distracted. Managing time and maintaining focus on a single task can be challenging, but not insurmountable.

- **Impulsivity and Decision Making:** The spontaneity that leads to creative problem-solving can also result in impulsive decisions. Learning to pause and consider the ramifications can turn this impulsivity into calculated risk taking.

- **Inconsistency in Performance:** The variability in focus can lead to inconsistent work performance. Recognizing patterns and creating structured routines can mitigate this issue, ensuring high productivity.

Using ADHD to Embrace the Chaos

In my journey, I learned to embrace the chaos that comes with ADHD.

I remember walking into a networking event, buzzing with the energy and chatter of hundreds of professionals. While many might find this overwhelming, I saw it as a playground for my (occasionally) hyperactive mind. My ability to hop from conversation to conversation, drawing connections between disparate topics and people, was not just a coping mechanism—it was my superpower. Think of the now-famous Zach Galifianakis meme from *The*

Hangover, surrounded by mathematical equations on screen as he counts cards at Caesars Palace.

Inevitably, though, I am somewhat of an outlier. Even the most extroverted among us do not necessarily look at a networking event as a *de facto* scavenger hunt. For the introverted crowd, the situation I just described sounds akin to a colonoscopy.

As we've discussed, there is zero expectation that after reading this book, you will love networking events and industry mixers as much as I do. However, the bottom line is that establishing connections and building a strong network is paramount in any professional position.

To do that, we can all lean into our ADHD just a little. Here are some simple exercises:

- **Wear an outfit that makes you feel and look fantastic:** As Coco Chanel said: "Dress shabbily and they remember the dress; dress impeccably and they remember the woman (or man)."

- **Develop an archetype of a person you would like to meet:** What is their background? Who would they like to meet? What are they looking to accomplish from a gathering like this one?

- **Have an imaginary conversation with that person in the mirror before you leave to go to the event:** Role playing with yourself ahead of the event to think through how you want the conversation to go, will then make the actual interaction easier.

- **Get to the event early and introduce yourself to one person:** Standing in line for a nametag, drink, or food provides a great opportunity to chat up a stranger. It forges connection more naturally than jumping right into the conversation circle, especially if you're more tentative at these types of larger social events.

- **Have three conversations with new people:** If you can leave the gathering with three new connections, then the event will have been a success for you. Once you meet the first new person, you can flex your new skill of gracefully extracting yourself from a conversation to meet two more people.

- **Act as the host:** Like we talked about earlier in the demonstrating curiosity chapter, take ownership of the event, even if it's not your party! Help people to their seats, ask them if they need a drink, etc. These small gestures will help others feel more at ease, and in the process, so will you.

A CREATIVE'S PROFESSIONAL SUPERPOWER

Will these mindset shifts mean that you automatically look forward to networking events as much as I do? Of course not.

However, the goal is to adopt enough simple tricks and tactics that even the most reserved introverts can at least tolerate these events enough to build connections and, by extension, their careers.

Jason Dominy is a strategist running his own marketing consultancy, Flat Six Services. Jason and I were first connected in 2013 when we worked together at Engauge, a marketing services agency. Like me, Jason has also been diagnosed with ADHD, and similarly has found there are unique professional benefits that come with the ability to shift focus quickly, especially in a field, like marketing, where creativity and unorthodox thinking are the names of the game.

"ADHD has been a superpower professionally," he said. "It has made me more creative, empathetic, strategic, and willing to try things outside the box. These attributes have helped me tremendously in the marketing world, creating fun campaigns informed by strategy that is guided by data and insights."

Jason knows he needs to be disciplined about establishing structure, so that he can actually follow through on the initiatives that come out of his extemporaneous thinking.

"It certainly requires me to instill systems to assure success at work," he shares. "Lists and reminders help keep me on task and allow me to take full advantage of the creativity and inspiration ADHD adds to my life. It also helps me create and foster a more positive community that is led by empathy."

ADDING "ROCKET FUEL" TO ADHD

In Gino Wickman's and Mark C. Winter's book *Rocket Fuel*, the longtime entrepreneurs draw the distinction between **Visionaries** (big-picture thinkers) and

Integrators (focused on practical execution). When these two roles collaborate well, they create "rocket fuel" for the business, as they serve complementary roles.

"As a visionary, you have lots of ideas," Wickman and Winters write. "You typically have ten news ideas a week. Many of them may not be so good, or at least not a fit with the company's primary focus. However, a few are absolutely brilliant. And those few great ideas keep the organization growing.

"An Integrator," the authors add, "has the unique ability to harmoniously integrate the major functions of the business, run the organization, and manage the day-to-day issues that arise. The Integrator is the glue that holds the people, processes, systems, priorities, and the strategy of the company together."[2]

Visionaries are critical to creating new companies, as well as helping young organizations grow. They generate an abundance of new ideas, an incredible currency for any organization. Those with ADHD are typically characterized by creativity, spontaneity, and a penchant for high energy in social situations. All of these are great ingredients for starting

---

[2]   Wickman, Geno, and Winters, Mark C. *Rocket Fuel* (Dallas, Texas: Ben Bella Books, 2015), 4, 28.

a business, building a pipeline of clients, and connecting with a wide network of customers and colleagues in the organization's early stages to improve and refine the product.

Integrators, meanwhile, refine the plethora of schemes and suggestions coming from the Visionaries and provide structure to them. If we look at Visionaries as providing the creative spark, Integrators are the kindling that actually allows the flame to catch. Without them, the bonfire simply dies out, no matter how many times you strike a match.

Throughout my career, as a Visionary, I've been skilled at starting new ventures, but perhaps not always as skilled at finishing them. As a result, I have to align myself with people who are detail-oriented and capable of executing and delivering on those big-picture ideas. That's why my colleague Amanda M. Thompson, the president at Setup, has been so instrumental in our organization's success. As the Integrator, Amanda is able to provide the structure and framework for both bigger initiatives, as well as smaller, behind-the-scenes work.

For example, in the course of running a business, there are so many smaller, detail-oriented tasks that are not my strength—and quite frankly, my ADHD diagnosis doesn't help. Sitting down to complete technical tasks can be a real challenge for me, as I tend to wander to the next idea before the existing initiative is even fleshed out. Taking the time to sit down and look at the granular details of our company health care plans is about as enjoyable as chewing glass. However, as an organization, tasks like selecting health plans require a level of detail that is critical to the business, whether you find it interesting or not. And luckily for me, Amanda enjoys doing these types of projects.

This dynamic is far from uncommon. Those with ADHD often jump from idea to idea, providing inspiration for new initiatives. However, these new processes need structure and framework in order to develop—otherwise, there is no execution and these ideas will wither on the vine. Those with heightened creativity and a penchant for juggling lots of new priorities need to be intentional about aligning themselves with Integrators.

The point of this story is not about any actual ADHD diagnosis, but about leveraging some of the characteristics often associated with ADHD.

Impulsiveness and restlessness, most commonly associated with ADHD, have a negative connotation, but there are some real benefits that come with it as well, including creativity and outside-of-the-box problem-solving. These characteristics are integral for startups and young companies, which is why you often see founders leaning into these qualities.

Visionary founders need Integrators to help follow through on their multitude of ideas. Without my Visionary instincts (and a little dose of ADHD), Setup never would have gotten off the ground. At the same time, without Amanda, we never would have optimized our processes, and our growth would have stalled out a long time ago.

PRACTICAL WAYS TO HARNESS YOUR ADHD

Inevitably, I've had to learn some strategies of my own to compensate for the fact that I can become easily distracted.

As a founder and CEO, time management is essential, and that's one area in particular where those with ADHD do tend to struggle. Surrounding myself with colleagues like Amanda, who are naturally more process-driven, has helped me with the more exacting tasks of the business.

Even if you don't occasionally struggle with hyperactivity or paying attention, there are a series of practices that will help both Visionaries and Integrators increase productivity.

Here are some practical exercises I've used to leverage my ADHD in the business world:

- **Time-Blocking:** Allocate specific time slots for different tasks each day. This method helps in managing distractions and ensuring that you dedicate focused time to each task, making the most of your periods of hyper-focus.

- **Impulse Control Journal:** Keep a journal to record instances of impulsivity. Note the situation, your impulsive action, and the outcome. Reflecting on these instances will help you recognize patterns and learn when your impulsivity serves you well and when it doesn't.

- **Networking Strategy:** Before attending events, set clear objectives. Identify the types of individuals you want to connect with and prepare topics for discussion. This preparation allows you to channel your high energy and enthusiasm into productive networking.

Again, while ADHD is typically connected to poor attention spans and hyperactivity, there are incredible positives that also come with it that bring real value to any organization, if harnessed properly. In my case, it enabled me to lean into my interest in relationships and connecting individuals from all sorts of different backgrounds. My business would not exist without my atypical skillset.

On the flip side, those who are naturally more process-oriented may find that exhibiting more creativity and spontaneity helps them find solutions to complex problems. Much like the capabilities of Visionaries and Integrators complement each other to form "rocket fuel," individuals can benefit from adopting a more process-oriented mindset if they're naturally more creative, or those who are more structural thinkers can embrace more spontaneous solutions.

4

DEVELOPING DIPLOMACY

Diplomacy is essential in maintaining professional relationships. Diplomacy helps you navigate tricky social dynamics, resolve conflicts, and manage diverse personalities gracefully and tactfully. Becoming a good diplomat also makes you more valuable in a work or personal setting.

Diplomacy can strengthen connections and maintain long-term trust. There is an element of politics involved in becoming a good diplomat. I once mentioned to a friend that he was very good at politics within our workplace. He was immediately offended, thinking I was talking about the stereo-typical "office politics," which involves backstabbing, conniving, and gossiping. I quickly clarified that I was complimenting his ability to coach and bring together the right people to accomplish tasks. He is adept at the best aspects of politics, but perhaps I should have told him he is an excellent diplomat.

Becoming a better diplomat can help you make more connections, as well as manage them better.

EXHIBITING DIPLOMACY

Here is how this nuanced skill can help you manage each of the following areas in a more productive way.

- **Politics:** The best diplomats are adept at leveraging the best aspects of politics to help them navigate relationships. They think through who to involve in a critical meeting to accomplish something within their organization. They know when to coach someone who needs a morale boost or to supply direct feedback to someone who needs to be corrected. They plan for strategic conversations in advance and focus on outcomes while also considering the feelings of the others involved in the discussion. They also know when to ignore non-productive communication or find a better time to respond.

- **Timing:** Knowing when to speak and listen is just as crucial as the words themselves. This ability to read the room and understand unspoken dynamics is a skill that can be honed with practice. The more you engage in delicate conversations, the more you'll learn to pick up on cues indicating when someone is receptive to feedback, or is too emotionally charged to process it constructively.

- **Compromise:** Another critical element of diplomacy is the art of compromise. You don't always need to have the final word or push your agenda at all costs. The most successful diplomats understand that finding common ground, even if it means giving up a little, can lead to more robust, sustainable professional and personal relationships in the long term. It's not about winning or losing, but maintaining the relationship's integrity. A well-executed compromise leads to more goodwill and trust than any singular victory could.

- **Principles:** Don't mistake the ability to compromise for being a pushover. Diplomacy requires balancing empathy and assertiveness. You must be firm in your principles but flexible in your approach. This is especially important when mediating between conflicting parties. It's your role to ensure both sides feel heard, respected, and valued, but that doesn't mean allowing one side to steamroll the other. Sometimes, the best diplomatic approach is to create space for each person to voice their concerns while guiding the conversation toward a productive and fair resolution.

- **Questions:** One of the most effective tools in a diplomat's arsenal is asking the right questions. When conflicts arise or tensions escalate, well-placed questions can help defuse the situation and uncover the root cause of the issue. Instead of focusing on what's wrong or what went wrong, shift the conversation toward solutions. For example, asking, "How do you see this working out for both of us?" signals your interest in a collaborative resolution and encourages the other person to think constructively.

- **Flexibility:** It's essential to understand that diplomacy isn't a one-size-fits-all skill. What works with one person might not work with another, and part of your job as a connector is to tailor your approach to the personalities and communication styles of the people involved. This adaptability will make you a more effective bridge between people and various groups and stakeholders.

After college, I worked as an Assistant Manager for Abercrombie & Fitch in New Orleans, Louisiana, and then went to work for Eddie Bauer in the same role. Eddie Bauer offered me a job to move to Jackson Hole, Wyoming, to become the store manager there. While there, I had a fantastic boss, Michael Wilson, who was the district manager for all of the stores in the Western region. He was an excellent leader who knew how to bring the right people on my team into the conversation and when to focus one-on-one with me.

I will never forget the sage advice he gave me during a one-on-one coaching conversation: "Keep your knees bent."

Initially, I did not understand the reference. Michael was an avid skier, and this is an important tip for skiing. I, however, did not understand the application for my business career. He went on to explain that the reason to keep your knees bent on the ski slope was to prepare to make a sudden turn when the surrounding conditions change.

In business, "keeping your knees bent" means being ready to pivot rapidly as conditions change in your environment.

The goal of diplomacy is not just to resolve conflicts, but to build and maintain trust over time. When people see that you can handle difficult situations with grace and fairness, they'll be more likely to turn to you in the future—not just for conflict resolution, but for guidance, mentorship, and advice. This strengthens your position as a trusted connector and enhances your ability to make meaningful introductions that stand the test of time.

EXHIBITING FLEXIBILITY IN DIPLOMACY

These diplomatic principles play out in real workplace scenarios every day. Sometimes flexibility means changing the structure, and other times it means changing how you show up within that structure. Let me share two examples.

Madeline is a member of the Setup team. She's a professional improvisation actor and teacher on the side. Most of her improv career happens late at night—often working shows that begin at 10 p.m. Since Madeline has an entire life outside of her day job at Setup, my team and I have had to be flexible with her—especially when it comes to the hours she works. Madeline often begins her workday much later in the morning, but she tends to work after the rest of my team has checked out for the day. My team trusts that she is putting in the effort and the hours to excel and ensure that Setup is benefiting from her creative talents and hard work.

Diplomatic flexibility also extends to how and when we communicate, particularly when delivering difficult feedback.

Melissa M. Proctor began her career at Turner Broadcasting as an intern and worked her way up to become the Vice President of Brand Marketing & Content at Upwave, which was a startup station within Turner focused on health and wellness. When Turner shut down Upwave, Melissa was recruited to work for the Atlanta Hawks as their VP of Brand Strategy. She was then promoted to Senior Vice President of Strategy, and ultimately to EVP and Chief Marketing Officer for the Atlanta Hawks and State Farm Arena.

I believe that Melissa has progressed rapidly in her career largely due to her ability to navigate politics within the organizations she serves. She once shared a story with me about a boss that she had while managing a division of the Cartoon Network within Turner Broadcasting. The boss seemed to be missing some cultural awareness that was critical to managing her team well. Melissa's boss was very Type A and always asked sharp, probing questions of her team as they were preparing for a big meeting. While the boss thought the meeting went great, Melissa could tell from the team's deadpan response that they did not receive the communication well. Melissa asked her boss for a coaching moment. Of course, the boss thought Melissa was asking for advice, but it turned out that Melissa wanted to advise her boss. Offering unsolicited advice to the boss was a risk for Melissa, especially as a junior team member, but it was well received.

In that moment, Melissa was empowered because of their strong relationship, which helped her overcome a nervous situation. In the end, Melissa's feedback helped the boss improve, as she changed her communication style for the better to build stronger bonds with her team.

The immediacy of Melissa's communication made her coaching effective. It is crucial that this kind of critical feedback happens in the moment and not too long after the incident that requires feedback.

Melissa has also shared with me that for her, developing diplomacy is about building trust with her team by showing up as her authentic self at work. Melissa makes it a point not to "put on a corporate face" despite being a C-level executive. She intentionally shows her human side to the team by celebrating their wins and empathizing with their challenges—professional and personal. Melissa makes it clear to her team that she is the same person inside the office as she is at home with her daughter or out with friends.

By honing your diplomatic skills, you'll manage conflicts more effectively and foster an environment where collaboration and trust thrive. The more you practice, the more natural it will become to easily navigate complex social dynamics, helping you unlock even more profound levels of connection and success in your personal and professional life.

EMBRACING VULNERABILITY

Vulnerability isn't always the first word that comes to mind when people think about connecting with others. Often, we believe that to build relationships, especially in professional settings, we need to be flawless, confident, and in possession of all the answers. But the truth is that vulnerability is one of the most powerful tools you can use to forge meaningful and lasting connections.

At its core, vulnerability is about being open, honest, and authentic. It means showing up as your true self without pretense, admitting when you don't know something, and sharing your feelings—even when it feels uncomfortable. Being vulnerable allows you to create deeper bonds, inviting others to do the same.

When we think of vulnerability, we often equate it with weakness or a lack of confidence, but the opposite is true. **Vulnerability requires courage.** It's about being brave enough to drop the armor and let people see the real you. This openness builds trust, which is the foundation of all great connections, both personal and professional.

WHY VULNERABILITY MATTERS IN BUILDING CONNECTIONS

When you're vulnerable, you create a space where others feel safe to be vulnerable, too. It's a signal that you're not here to impress or dominate the conversation, but to connect on a human level. This is especially critical in business, where connections can often feel transactional.

Here's the reality: we all have imperfections, fears, and doubts. Allowing someone to see yours breaks down the barriers that often exist in relationships, opening the door to empathy and mutual understanding. Whether you're meeting someone for the first time or deepening an existing relationship, vulnerability creates an emotional resonance that can't be achieved through surface-level interactions.

Consider the difference between these two scenarios:

1. You walk into a meeting with a new colleague, determined to project confidence. You only talk about your successes and avoid admitting to any challenges.

2. In a different meeting, you candidly share a challenge you've been working through and ask for input.

In the first scenario, the conversation stays shallow, and the colleague may feel disconnected from you because they can't relate to perfection. In the second scenario, you open the door to dialogue and collaboration. By sharing something real, you make it easier for them to do the same, building rapport and trust. I will expand on this idea further in the next section.

In 2004, I met a young woman on a blind date. After a six-month courtship, I proposed, and we married in 2006. In 2010, we welcomed girl/boy twins to our family. In late 2022, after nineteen years together, it became clear that our marriage was no longer working for either of us. In 2023, we divorced. While our separation and divorce were relatively amicable, these types of life changes are never easy. Unwinding nineteen years together took its toll on me personally as I had to face a new reality of life without a spouse, while still co-parenting two teenagers.

It was clear to my Setup team during this period that I was hurting and distracted. I was trying to balance the divorce process, parenting, running Setup, and fulfilling other commitments I had made. Being the CEO of a company is challenging and can feel lonely at any point. These dynamics are exacerbated when you no longer have the support of a spouse with whom you are accustomed to sharing and leaning on.

In the middle of the divorce process, I promoted Amanda, our Chief Operating Officer, to President, and her first question for me (rightly so) was, "Where are you going?" I assured her that I was not going anywhere and that I would get my head back in the game by recommitting my attention to the success of the company.

Of course, as Founder and CEO, I was the driver of the vision and set the course for the company. For a short period of time, I felt rudderless. I openly talked about some of the challenges I faced rather than bottling them up. Regular conversations with my team, especially Amanda, led to their understanding of the challenges and emotions I was dealing with. Setting the vision for our company, while also navigating a divorce process, was difficult. I really couldn't manage it on my own. I came to lean on Amanda for support personally and professionally, and it ultimately fostered more mutual trust as colleagues.

In retrospect, Amanda agrees it was a turning point in our relationship as company leaders. "Once we established that I didn't really want to hear details of your dating life," Amanda joked, "we have had and continue to have productive, honest conversations. Maybe we would have anyway, but the growth you've had since your divorce has made us closer."

Amanda and my entire team stepped up to allow me the space to heal from the challenges of such a painful life transition. I believe that vulnerably sharing my feelings and emotions with my team caused them to see me as a human and want to help me. That deeper level of trust ultimately benefited the company as a whole.

Today, in my role as founder and Amanda's role as president, we work together closely on many different initiatives and projects. While I certainly would never have set out for my divorce to be a seminal moment in our relationship as coworkers, it has undoubtedly been beneficial. Tackling problems like budgets, project scope, and resource allocation doesn't seem daunting when the other person has supported you when you needed them.

"You seem more likely to talk about issues with me that are bugging you about Setup, me, and the team," Amanda said. "Even if you don't like what I'm saying, you seem more open to listening, digesting, and determining a path forward."

WHEN PERSONAL EXPERIENCE TRANSFORMS PROFESSIONAL RELATIONSHIPS

Stacey Tank is the CEO of Bespoke Beauty Brands. Throughout her career, she has been a dynamic leader at a number of different corporations, including serving as Chief Executive at Home Depot Installation Services, as well as the Chief Transformation Officer at Heineken.

Stacey first started in finance and communications at General Electric, working in a high-pressure, fast-paced environment. As a new mother, this was a difficult position to navigate. She started to think about opportunities that emphasized balance around people and performance. Around the same time, she was forced to make a decision around her personal health, and the learnings from that situation have impacted her to this day.

In her late twenties, Stacey learned that she was a carrier for the BRCA gene making her risk for breast or ovarian cancer high. She also watched her mother undergo stage-four breast cancer, with multiple recurrences and rounds of chemotherapy and radiation. As a result of her mother's medical procedures and surgeries, Stacey wanted to avoid that for herself, as well as her family. She made the preemptive decision to have a prophylactic bilateral mastectomy.

Through this process, Stacey became connected with Bright Pink, an organization which expands the impact of life-saving breast and ovarian health interventions. They also connected her with other women who had undergone that same procedure. Stacey admitted that she would have been overwhelmed by the process, and what it meant for her own body image, if she had been forced to do it on her own.

When she searched online for information, the results showed post-cancer mastectomy images of much older women—nothing that helped a young woman in her twenties envision her own journey. "Bright Pink was amazing because I got together with young ladies who had made the same choice and they were so generous about things that were very private and very vulnerable—their bodies, their scars, their relationships with their partners, siblings, and children. They're the most intimate things."

The turning point for Stacey actually came in a Starbucks. Still wrestling with the decision of whether to have the surgery, a woman from Bright Pink took Stacey into the bathroom of the coffee shop and showed Stacey her own mastectomy scars. That instance of radical generosity and vulnerability gave Stacey the courage she needed.

"It was like, *I can do this*," Stacey said. "I thought, *This is totally OK*." I don't think it's an exaggeration to say she saved my life."

The experience proved to be a turning point in Stacey's life. She was motivated to be more open and pay it forward to other women undergoing breast cancer. More than just a personal transformation, though, it fundamentally changed the attitude she carried professionally.

The experience transformed how Stacey showed up professionally, helping her shed the "buttoned up" persona she'd maintained since childhood.

This new outlook was especially apparent years later. In a similar dynamic to what I experienced sharing my divorce with close members of my team, Stacey had to be more open professionally as her family navigated another challenging medical issue.

Years later, when her family faced another medical challenge, Stacey didn't calculate whether to be vulnerable with her team—she just was. She shared what was happening and asked for advice. "We just needed help and they made me feel safe to be able to say that," she said. With so much on her mind, she couldn't contemplate any other way to show up.

Stacey added that one of the reasons it helped others connect with her was that she was looked at as a mother and a human, not a hard-charging corporate executive. It changed the way she related to members on her team who weren't as proximate to her. In a way, they got to see beneath the mask.

"It's a great reminder to be intentional," Stacey said. "It's not that I wasn't trying to be, but taking the extra time to let people peek underneath your own circus tent helps you to connect as humans and find a ton of common ground."

Stories like Stacey's reveal why vulnerability matters beyond the immediate moment. When leaders show up as whole humans, they unlock something larger.

HOW VULNERABILITY ENHANCES PROFESSIONAL GROWTH

Vulnerability isn't just about emotional openness; it's also a catalyst for growth. Admitting you don't have all the answers invites fresh perspectives, collaboration, and unexpected solutions. One of the biggest obstacles to personal and professional growth is the fear of failure or appearing inadequate. Yet, some of the most successful people in the world embrace vulnerability, openly acknowledging their mistakes and failures as stepping stones to success.

Think of the leaders who inspire you the most. Chances are, they don't project dominance—they admit their missteps, take responsibility for them, and share their lessons. In the business world, people want to work with those whom they trust, and trust comes from seeing someone's real, imperfect self.

When you embrace vulnerability, you tell others it's okay to be human when making connections. You signal that you value authenticity over perfection. This is especially important when making introductions. It's not just about pairing the proper skills or expertise. It's about creating connections between people who are willing to be open, honest, and engaged with one another.

In late 2007, I took a job as VP of Business Development and Marketing for a digital agency called Spunlogic (which was later acquired by Engauge). I had transitioned from selling a digital product for KnowledgeStorm (now TechTarget) to selling marketing services. My transition from selling products to selling services was initially a disaster. I quickly found that I was failing at my job, which required knowledge specific to the marketing industry, as well as much more attention to detail than I previously needed in my role at KnowledgeStorm.

Because I was falling short of the expectations of my peers (VP of Client Services, VP of Strategy, and VP of Research and Innovation), I was called into a meeting with them and the CEO to outline all of the ways I was failing in my new role, including lack of understanding of the roles within the agency, what the teams within the agency do, attention to details for proposals and pitches, and respect for the time and effort it would take for others to "fix" my mistakes. It was clear to me how serious it was... either I figured things out, or I was gone. Much to my peers' surprise, I took their feedback without defensiveness and worked tirelessly over the next few months to build the missing skills and their trust.

My colleagues, who were previously concerned about my ability to succeed in the role, became my biggest advocates as they saw me putting in the work to achieve the success they were hoping for. I went on to help the agency grow by shepherding in some of the most important clients, including Newell Brands, AMC Theatres, Chick-fil-A, Cisco Systems, Hershey's, and many others—eventually reaching over $40 million in annual revenue before selling to Publicis Group in 2013.

I frequently (and publicly) tell how I was almost fired in early 2008. I share the story because it demonstrates vulnerability. Those who hear the story often respond that they can relate to the stress I must have felt and appreciate my willingness to share my shortcomings.

As the Founder and CEO of Setup, when someone on my team struggles to learn something new or achieve a seemingly impossible task, I routinely reshare my struggles in my last job. My message to them: everyone faces moments where they have to prove themselves, and those challenges can become defining opportunities for growth.

PRACTICAL WAYS TO EMBRACE VULNERABILITY

Now that we understand why vulnerability is powerful, how do we begin to practice it? Here are some actionable steps:

- **Admit when you don't know something:** Be open about your knowledge gaps instead of bluffing your way through a conversation. It allows others to share their expertise and helps you learn from their experiences.

- **Ask for help:** This one can be particularly tough, especially if you pride yourself on being independent. Asking for help fosters collaboration and deepens relationships because people appreciate the opportunity to contribute.

- **Share your failures:** Don't be afraid to discuss your mistakes in a meeting or a casual conversation. Sharing what went wrong—and how you bounced back—can be incredibly relatable and valuable to others.

- **Use "I don't know" as a strength:** There's a misconception that a leader or professional must have all the answers. In reality, saying "I don't know" can make you more relatable and trustworthy. It shows that you value learning over pretending.

- **Acknowledge your emotions:** Being open about your feelings can deepen your connection with others, whether you're excited, frustrated, or even nervous. You don't have to overshare, but a little emotional transparency goes a long way.

- **Give genuine compliments:** Vulnerability isn't always about sharing weaknesses. Sometimes, it's about expressing positive emotions like gratitude or admiration. Letting someone know how they've impacted you or acknowledging their strengths can create a strong connection.

- **Self-deprecation:** Telling a story about someone else's flaws rarely engenders trust and empathy. However, sharing your own inadequacies and missteps can indeed build emotional bonds.

If vulnerability is so powerful, why do so many of us shy away? The answer is fear—fear of being judged, rejected, or seen as less capable. But here's the thing: vulnerability is not a weakness; it's a strength.

Start small. You don't need to be vulnerable with everyone all the time. Identify a few trusted colleagues or friends with whom you feel safe being more open. Share something you might typically keep to yourself—a challenge, a question, a doubt. Over time, you'll see how vulnerability deepens those relationships and encourages others to be vulnerable in return. Of course, sharing vulnerability requires some thoughtfulness and nuance.

THE LONG-TERM IMPACT OF VULNERABILITY ON RELATIONSHIPS

When you consistently embrace vulnerability, you'll notice that your connections become more prolific and more meaningful. People are drawn to authenticity. They appreciate those brave enough to admit they don't have it all figured out. Vulnerability allows you to build relationships based on trust, understanding, and mutual respect.

Abby England (whom I mentioned in Chapter 2) also found that honesty and vulnerability helped her through her own divorce. Unsurprisingly, she felt incredibly vulnerable during a difficult period of her life, and people responded with compassion and empathy, which led to a deepening of the relationship.

"My biggest learning post-divorce was this: I had been investing 99% of my energy in one person. When that relationship imploded, I redirected that energy into many people, and the ROI was tenfold."

"As Brene Brown says," Abby added, "'Vulnerability is the last thing you want to show, but the first thing people look for.' I've become more open, honest, and vulnerable about my personal situation on social media, and every time I post something, someone from my past reaches out and says, 'I'm going through that too.'"

In my own experience, some of the most potent connections I've made have come from moments of vulnerability. When I share a personal story or admit a mistake, people often respond with their own experiences, leading to a deeper bond and mutual appreciation. These connections aren't fleeting. They're the kinds of relationships that last for years and serve as a strong foundation for professional and personal growth.

Ultimately, embracing vulnerability means letting go of the need to be perfect and embracing the beauty of being human.

It means understanding that our imperfections make us relatable and that genuine connection comes from showing up as we are—flaws and all.

When you lead with vulnerability, you create space for others to do the same. You build more profound, authentic relationships beyond the surface level. And in a world where so much feels transactional, these connections will set you apart.

By practicing vulnerability in your personal and professional life, you will create meaningful connections and experience the joy and fulfillment of being your true self. And that, in the end, makes all the difference.

MAKING MEANINGFUL INTRODUCTIONS

I have found over and over that being generous with your connections, by making introductions for others, pays dividends in the long run. Making meaningful introductions is an art—thoughtfully understanding the needs, interests, and potential synergies between people.

At its core, an introduction is more than just sharing a name and contact information. It's about fostering a relationship that could benefit both parties, ensuring that each person feels valued and that the introduction serves a purpose.

UNDERSTANDING THE PURPOSE BEHIND THE INTRODUCTION

Before introducing two people, it's essential to consider the *why*.

What do you hope will come out of this connection? Maybe one person has a skill set or service the other needs, or perhaps they share a common interest that can lead to future collaboration.

Introductions can be for business, friendship, mentorship, or a shared passion. **The introduction is meaningful because of the intention behind it.** You aren't simply passing people along to each other. You're helping them forge a relationship that could be mutually beneficial.

Darrah Brustein is an executive coach to C-suite leaders. One of the keys to the success of Darrah's career has been her network, and as she coaches entrepreneurs and executives, she stresses to them that their network supports everything they do. She is a master at not only building her own network but also building *other people's* networks. Not surprisingly, building people's networks is an activity Darrah in-trinsically enjoys for its own sake, not just looking at it through the lens of what she could receive from it.

"I look at the world as a puzzle of people and op-portunities to piece together," she said. "It's fun like a scavenger hunt, and if one plus one can equal more than the sum of its parts, that's wonderful. They say there's no selfless act, and this is included. Our brains love the positive feelings that come from doing it."

The Power of Context

Context is vital when making an introduction. Providing background information about each person ensures that the introduction doesn't fall flat. This goes beyond a generic, "you two should meet." Instead, give each person a reason to connect with the other. For example, if introducing a business owner to a marketing expert, highlight the specific marketing challenges the business owner faces and explain how the marketing expert's unique experi-ence could be a perfect fit.

A successful introduction would be something like this: "Sarah, I'd like to introduce you to Ben. Ben is a marketing strategist with deep experience in e-commerce, especially within small businesses like yours. I think you'll find his approach to digital marketing incredibly helpful as you're looking to expand your online sales. Ben, Sarah runs a fantastic local retail business and wants to grow her digital presence. I think you two will have a lot to talk about."

Notice how the introduction provides context and highlights what each person brings to the table. This helps both parties see the value in connecting and gives them something concrete to discuss in their first interaction.

Timing Matters

Not all introductions need to happen right away. Sometimes, waiting for the right moment can make a world of difference. Timing matters because the person you're introducing may not be ready to engage, or the situation might not yet call for the connection. Assess whether the timing is conducive to both parties and if both are able to make the most of the introduction.

For example, someone in the middle of a major project may not be in the right headspace to focus on a new opportunity or connection. By waiting until the timing is right, you increase the likelihood that the introduction will be meaningful.

The Personal Touch

When you make an introduction, it's not just about the logistics. It's also about creating a moment where two people feel seen and understood. Adding personal touches, like sharing a memorable anecdote or highlighting something you admire about each person, makes the introduction feel more genuine.

For example, when introducing a colleague who's an exceptional designer, you might say, "I've worked with Lisa for years, and she has this incredible knack for turning abstract ideas into visually stunning designs. Her ability to communicate brand stories visually is beyond comparison."

By adding personal details, you show that you've taken the time to understand each person, making the introduction less transactional and more human.

Darrah adds that the more personal and genuine the introduction feels, the better. "Don't overcomplicate it," she said. "You've likely made hundreds of introductions in your life casually. Let it be natural."

It's okay if you don't find making introductions second nature. Having a simple email introduction template where you can fill in the blanks with information that gives each party enough background, context, and reason for the introduction can work as a first step. And then, just like all other skills, the task will become easier with practice and repetition.

Follow Up and Facilitation

Your job as a connector doesn't end with the introduction. Meaningful connections often need a little help to take off. Following up with both parties after an introduction can ensure the connection progresses positively. This doesn't mean you need to micromanage the relationship, but a simple, "How did your conversation go?" shows your investment in their success.

Sometimes, introductions can benefit from an additional nudge. If the initial connection doesn't seem to spark immediately, it's okay to facilitate a follow-up or provide more context. Often, people are busy, and they may need a gentle reminder or more information to see the full value of the connection.

CREATING LONG-TERM IMPACT

Introductions can have ripple effects that go beyond the immediate conversation. A thoughtful connection today might result in opportunities, collaborations, or friendships. You're planting the seed by making a meaningful introduction. Even if the connection doesn't immediately produce results, it could lead to something valuable down the road.

People remember who introduced them to key individuals in their lives. When you are intentional about making thoughtful introductions, you build a reputation as someone who brings value to relationships. You're not just introducing people to fill a void—you're enhancing their networks and helping them achieve their goals.

This applies to professional and personal relationships. In fact, one of Darrah's most memorable connections had nothing to do with her business. "My older brother AJ is a lifetime fan of the Miami Dolphins, as well as a talented photographer. While at a retreat in Italy, I met a man who is the NFL's official photographer. As he shared about his work, I joked that my brother would love to experience his job for a day. Without hesitation, he offered to invite my brother to join him at a game. So, I did, and the next Monday Night Football game when the Dolphins played, my brother got all-access press passes to watch and shoot the game with him. He said he's never had a better gift."

Her brother received a priceless experience, and for Darrah, there was incredible fulfillment in facilitating that once-in-a-lifetime moment, simply out of her interest in fostering relationships.

"I, too, got the gift of seeing him live out a dream he didn't even know he had, simply by connecting the dots."

In addition to creating once-in-a-lifetime memories, making meaningful introductions can indeed be life-changing. Several years ago, I introduced my longtime friend from college, Rachel Kuramoto (who wrote the foreword), to my former colleague Jeff Hilimire, the founder and president of Spunlogic (later Engauge).

By the time of the introduction, in early 2018, each of them was running their own company. Rachelle served as the Founder and CEO of Watchword Brand, an agency focused on branding and content marketing, while Jeff was running Dragon Army, a mobile-first digital agency. A year later, after the introduction, Dragon Army acquired Watchword to better serve clients through its web, mobile, content, and brand offerings.

As it turns out, one of the services Watchword offered, which was then folded into Dragon Army, was book editing. Together, Jeff and Rachelle founded Ripples Media, which is (of course) the publisher of record for the book you are holding in your hand.

So, when we talk about long-term impact, the initial connection I made ultimately led to the creation of a publisher for my very own book a decade later. (I could think of nobody better to write the foreword to this book than Rachelle.)

Fate indeed does have a funny way of working. However, when you are purposeful about the introductions you make and the relationships you create, they can pay unexpected dividends.

INTENTIONALITY IS KEY

The key to making meaningful introductions is intention. When you thoughtfully connect two people with a clear purpose, provide context, and facilitate the relationship, you are creating value. Think beyond the surface level of introductions and focus on making connections that benefit the people involved. Remember, it's not just about the introduction itself but about the long-term potential the introduction holds for both parties. While it cannot be all about this, the people you introduce are all the more likely to one day return the favor and make a great introduction for you.

The connections you help foster can bring immense joy, fulfillment, and success, not only for those whom you introduce but also for yourself.

Each meaningful introduction strengthens your own network while building the foundation for future opportunities you may not even imagine yet.

7

NURTURING A GROWTH MINDSET

A growth mindset is the belief that abilities can be developed with dedication and practice. I like the seed analogy: some seedlings pop right away; others need time, water, and care before they break through.

This outlook builds resilience and comfort with challenge. People who lean into it welcome feedback, treat setbacks as useful data, and keep looking for ways to get better and help others do the same.

It's also the engine behind meaningful connection. With a growth mindset, obstacles turn into stepping stones.

You're more likely to follow up after a lukewarm first meeting, to retry an introduction that didn't land to keep learning what helps two people click. That shift reduces the fear of rejection and frees you to build relationships that last.

And it doesn't stop at work. This mindset improves how you show up at home and with friends, sharpens your judgment when problems get messy, and nudges you to keep growing. Every conversation, every introduction, every new experience becomes a chance to expand your world and invite others into it.

ENVISIONING YOUR IDEAL SELF

Adam Albrecht is the author of *What Does Your Fortune Cookie Say?*, a book aimed at helping individuals maximize their potential through positive thinking. Adam started his career as a copywriter for the agency Cramer-Krasselt before advancing all the way to Chief Creative Officer at Engauge, where he and I worked together from 2008 to 2014. Adam then started his own agency, The Weaponry, in 2016, where he serves as founder and CEO.

Adam's career is a testament to his growth mindset. He looks at adversity as opportunity and continually looks for new ways to improve, regardless of success or evolution.

"The first step to developing a growth mindset is to visualize the best version of yourself," he said. "Imagine the greatest version of yourself you can conceive of. That is your ideal self. What you are today is your real self. It is the version of you that you have already realized or attained. Now, your job is to simply put in the effort to close the gap between your real self and your ideal self." I feel that is easier said than done, but it is an aspirational goal to try to close that gap.

Adam adds that there's another key feature of nurturing a growth mindset: curiosity.

"Those with a fixed mindset believe their knowledge, skills, abilities, and limitations are fixed and unchanging," he said. "People with a growth mindset believe that they are continuously growing, evolving, and improving—which sounds way more hopeful."

When you embrace both the vision of who you want to become and the curiosity to keep learning, you create a powerful engine for personal transformation. With this mindset, every interaction can be a stepping stone toward your ideal self.

THE AUDACITY OF A TRY

Every year, I buy my entire Setup team tickets to attend TEDxAtlanta to provide "brain fertilizer" to fuel their creativity and develop new ideas for the next year. In 2025, we had the great fortune to hear George F. Baker III, an incredibly talented muralist, speak. George described how his career evolved from a graphic designer to a muralist—now that he has completed more than 50 murals. He talked about his father's initial skepticism about his choice as a designer and muralist as a profession. When his father finally experienced one of George's completed murals in person, George shared that his father welled up with pride at seeing the fruits of his labor–particularly knowing that George was paid to do the work.

One of the biggest drivers of success for George as a muralist has been the adoption of his own growth mindset. While these points specifically relate to painting, we can "draw" larger themes into our own lives. He posited that you can always paint over it. In other words, you can always take a stab at something and then fix it if it does not work out.

He went on to say that there is "the beauty of a try." **You can do anything with effort, time, and study.** George loves the idea of giving someone an opportunity to try on their new identity and that we should *reward audacity*. This growth mindset obviously has applications to building meaningful connections. When you approach relationships with George's philosophy, that you can always try again and that there's beauty in the attempt itself, reaching out and trying to connect with others should be celebrated.

HOW A GROWTH MINDSET LED ME TO ENTREPRENEURSHIP

After Engauge was sold to Publicis Groupe in 2013, I had six job offers, mostly from marketing agencies with knowledge of how, in my role as SVP of Marketing and Business Development, I helped Engauge grow to over $43 million in annual revenue. All the potential employers wanted me to help them grow similarly.

While trying to decide which offer to accept, I had breakfast with a mentor, Genevieve Bos, who pointed out that these agencies wanted me to bring in over 90% of the revenue but give me 5–10% equity in the company. She instead suggested that I start my own marketing agency.

It was an insightful point of feedback. My interest was not in building websites, creating social media content, or email marketing; my true passion was in matchmaking. I loved the chase *between* the agency and the client.

That conversation with her triggered a calling toward entrepreneurship that I hadn't otherwise considered. After that discussion, I had an epiphany that I could be a fractional business development resource for multiple agencies. This idea formed the basis of what would eventually become Setup. **I literally created a company out of leveraging my skill of matching people together.**

A great example of how this process would play out came shortly thereafter. I had discussions with the Director of Marketing for Cartoon Network, which was a client of Engauge. She was looking for a partner to help Cartoon Network with their mobile strategy, utilizing me as a sounding board to suggest a possible agency partner. I replied to her that while that agency was indeed a great agency, mobile wasn't its strength. Instead, I offered her the name of another agency to consider, one that did specialize in mobile.

This discussion formed the basis of what we do at Setup. We support marketers by connecting them with the best agencies for their specific needs. That first client ultimately chose the agency I had recommended, and the agency signed with Setup.

Our organization was born out of clients seeking the *right* connection. Later, I scheduled a meeting with one of the agencies that had been courting me. Once I laid out the plan for what Setup would be and how it would benefit the agency, they signed a contract a few days later. I incorporated Setup in early February of 2014. In the next few weeks, I got additional signed agreements from several other agencies. I immediately hired a former colleague I had recruited to Engauge, and the company was born!

A growth mindset is critical for entrepreneurship, but also for building deep networks. You are innately curious about other people's skills and talents, and how you can apply their learnings to better yourself, and your company.

Obviously, in my case, Setup was created as a matchmaking company, so the foundation of our business is predicated on having a deep network of clients and agencies that we can connect to each other. However, even if your business isn't geared to bring marketers together in the way that Setup is, as an entrepreneur, you are always in the business of growing your network. Your network helps connect you with potential clients, staff resources when a need arises on your internal team, and even a roster of sounding boards to solve problems. In order for companies to survive and grow, entrepreneurs have to constantly nurture and expand their networks.

It was never on my radar to start a company, but my natural curiosity and interest in people have been huge assets.

I have always been aware that I do not know it all, but have no problem seeking input and leaning on others. Time and again, I have enlisted the help of friends and mentors, including many of the people included in this book, to help me gather the necessary knowledge.

I also sought external education from organizations such as the Entrepreneur's Organization (EO). Joining the EO Atlanta Accelerator Program (designed to help smaller companies grow) early in the company's history made a huge impact on my understanding of how to develop the knowledge and skills needed to run a company. Each quarter, they host an all-day learning event with a different theme: Strategy, Cash, People, and Execution. Each session gives entrepreneurs the knowledge needed to level up to become one of the 4% of all companies that reach the hallowed $1 million in revenue mark. The three years I spent in this program, before graduating to become a full member of EO, were formative in helping me develop my own growth mindset.

GETTING IN THE RIGHT FRAME OF MIND

Like any skill, cultivating a growth mindset begins with intentionality. To shift into this mindset, you must first recognize and challenge any limiting beliefs that keep you from developing your potential.

- **Reframe Challenges as Opportunities:** Instead of seeing challenges as insurmountable obstacles, view them as chances to grow and learn. Every setback contains a lesson that can make you stronger.

- **Embrace Discomfort:** Growth requires stepping outside of your comfort zone. The more you expose yourself to new ideas, people, and experiences, the easier it becomes to navigate uncertainty with confidence.

- **Change Your Internal Dialogue:** Shift from self-defeating thoughts ("I'm not good at this") to growth-oriented statements ("I can learn this with time and effort").

- **Learn from Others:** Surround yourself with people who embody a growth mindset. Seek out mentors, read about successful individuals who have overcome challenges, and engage with those who inspire you to push beyond your limits.

- **Stay Curious:** Curiosity fuels growth. Ask questions, explore different perspectives, and remain open to learning from unexpected sources.

Taking Actions That Lead to Growth

A growth mindset thrives on action and continual improvement. Adam Albrect uses the analogy of a staircase.

"Your self-improvement journey is infinite," he said. "The level, step, or stair you are on today is simply where you are today. You have the ability to take another step up in any area of life by any measure you choose and at any time you choose."

In order to climb Adam's staircase, here are key steps to cultivate and reinforce this mindset:

- **Set Learning Goals, Not Just Achievement Goals:** Instead of focusing solely on accomplishments, prioritize goals that involve learning. For example, rather than aiming to "get ten new clients," set a goal to "learn three new strategies to attract clients."

- **Seek Constructive Feedback:** Feedback provides valuable insights for improvement. Instead of fearing criticism, actively seek input from colleagues, mentors, and peers whom you trust.

- **Practice Resilience:** Failure is an inevitable part of growth. Develop the ability to bounce back quickly by analyzing setbacks, extracting lessons, and applying them to future efforts.

- **Take Small, Consistent Steps:** Growth doesn't happen overnight. Incremental progress–taking one small step at a time–leads to lasting change. Regularly challenge yourself to stretch beyond what feels comfortable.

- **Teach Others What You Learn:** Sharing knowledge reinforces your own learning. Teaching someone else a concept you've mastered solidifies your understanding and strengthens your ability to apply it in new situations. Maybe even write a book about it one day.

Nurturing and Refining the Growth Mindset Skills

Maintaining a growth mindset is an ongoing process. Like a muscle, it must be exercised regularly to remain strong.

- **Make Reflection a Habit:** Take time to reflect on your experiences, challenges, and progress. Journaling or having regular self-check-ins can help track growth and reinforce positive habits.

- **Stay Adaptable:** Change is inevitable. Those with a growth mindset embrace shifts in circumstances, careers, and relationships, seeing them as opportunities for reinvention rather than sources of stress.

- **Celebrate Progress, Not Just Success:** Recognizing how far you've come fuels motivation. Acknowledge small wins and appreciate the lessons learned along the way.

- **Continuously Challenge Yourself:** As soon as you become comfortable, push yourself again. Whether it's learning a new skill, meeting new people, or tackling a difficult conversation, keep stretching your limits.

- **Reinforce Growth Through Connection:** Engage with people who inspire you to keep evolving. Surround yourself with individuals who challenge your thinking and encourage you to keep growing.

A GROWTH MINDSET
STARTS WITH HABITS

A growth mindset is not just about believing in potential. It's about taking intentional steps to unlock it.

"Imagine a version of yourself far greater and more capable than you are today," said Adam. "Then continuously work to close the gap. Allow yourself to be an amateur. Develop great habits that help you learn and grow. Experiment. Stay curious. Find someone who you want to be more like and discover their path. It will help you discover your own path to an even greater you."

By shifting your perspective, embracing challenges, and committing to continuous improvement, you can not only enhance your own life but also contribute to the success and growth of those around you. As you refine these skills, you will become a more effective connector and an invaluable collaborator.

Through practice and persistence, the ability to nurture a growth mindset will transform how you engage with the world, leading to deeper connections, greater success, and a more fulfilling life.

BUILDING LONG-TERM RELATIONSHIPS

> **Building a network isn't just about making initial connections—it's about nurturing relationships over time.**

S ome of the most valuable connections in your life and career will be the ones you've cultivated for years. Sometimes over decades. These relationships don't just provide professional advantages; they add richness, meaning, and depth to your personal and professional life. However, maintaining long-term relationships requires intentionality, effort, and a willingness to give more than you take.

Not all relationships carry the same weight, and that's okay. Some connections evolve into deep, personal relationships, while others remain professional and occasional. Both types serve a purpose:

- **Close connections:** These are the people you engage with frequently: colleagues, mentors, close friends, family, and trusted advisors. You lean on each other for advice, celebrate successes together, and provide mutual support.

- **Loose connections:** These are the individuals whom you may not talk to often but who remain part of your network. They can be former colleagues, past clients, industry peers, or acquaintances from various stages of life. They may even be LinkedIn connections that you ping occasionally. While they may not be a part of your daily or weekly interactions, they can still open doors, offer guidance, and provide fresh perspectives.

Loose connections are often underestimated. In reality, they are a powerful source of opportunity. Because they exist outside of your immediate circle, they have access to information, ideas, and networks that you don't. When nurtured correctly, these connections can prove to be invaluable.

David Nour is a longtime speaker and thought leader on the importance of business relationships. He's also served as an adjunct professor at the Goizueta Business School at Emory University and the Owen School of Management at Vanderbilt University. In his book *Relationship Economics*, David makes the point that there are three types of business relationships: functional, strategic, and lifetime.[3]

- **Functional:** Transactional and specific to a certain goal or objective.

- **Strategic:** A deep level of mutual trust built over a significant period of time, valuable to both parties.

- **Lifetime:** A long-term connection that extends beyond business and professional interests.

David outlines that, with the evolution of technology, transactional relationships continue to proliferate.

---

[3]   Nour, David. *Relationship Economics: Transform Your Most Valuable Business Contacts into Personal and Professional Success.* 3rd ed. Hoboken, NJ: Wiley, 2019.

In the age of AI, this dynamic will continue to grow. The key to success is looking at relationship-building through a longer-term lens, meaning that strategic and lifetime relationships will have the greatest impact on our professional and personal fulfillment.

"Savvy professionals find opportunities to monetize their business relationships through a long-term mutual *build and benefit* strategy," David writes.

If we view human connection through David's framework, building relationships is a long-term, lifelong pursuit. We derive the most benefit from relationships the longer we cultivate them and, quite frankly, work on them. If you boost your level of functional relationships, these connections could help with everything from a restaurant recommendation to even securing a new position. **The most personal value and deepest level of fulfillment comes from strategic and lifetime relationships, which often develop over a number of years.**

THE LONG-TERM PAYOFFS OF CLOSE PERSONAL CONTACTS

On many occasions, deep personal connections can provide tangible professional benefits. I have a close friend from college named Rob Funderburk. We were roommates as seniors, graduating in 1994 from Wake Forest University. We kept in touch periodically after college, but to my joyful surprise, our friendship helped me close a significant business deal—fifteen years later!

After college, Rob took a sales role at the Hershey Company, which is headquartered in Hershey, Pennsylvania. The company's portfolio of brands includes Hershey's, Reese's, Mr. Goodbar, Kit Kat, Ice Breakers, and many other candies. Rob worked there for sixteen years in a sales role, moving around to a number of different cities, but working in their main Pennsylvania headquarters from 2003 to 2005. Rob was always an affable guy and built strong relationships throughout the organization.

In 2009, while leading business development at Engauge, we were pitching Hershey's as a potential client. I reached out to Rob for the right contact there, and he connected me with the marketing executive's assistant. During my conversation with her, I casually mentioned, "My college roommate Rob has worked for Hershey for a long time." This was more than fifteen years after we'd graduated together.

She immediately responded, "I knew Rob when he worked here in Hershey, and he's fantastic. I'm not supposed to give anybody a meeting with Steve (the VP of Marketing Excellence), but if you're Rob's college roommate, I'll give you a meeting with Steve."

She immediately put us on the calendar. Soon thereafter, our agency President, VP of Strategy, and I went to Hershey's to pitch Steve and his deputy, the Director of Advertising. Following that initial meeting, we won business with eleven Hershey Company product lines.

As a direct effect of maintaining a relationship with Rob, and Rob maintaining his relationship with the assistant at Hershey's, these connections paid off as revenue for Engauge (and for me). As established earlier, the old saying goes, "*Your network is your net worth.*" That proved true in this situation, because I personally received a sales commission from the business we won—earnings made possible by my connection with Rob.

OCCASIONS FOR REACHING OUT TO LOOSE CONNECTIONS

In my case, Rob and I did stay in touch after college, which was a main reason I mentioned him during my initial conversations with the Hershey's executives.

However, not all connections have to be close in order to be valuable. More often than not, position referrals get passed on from a friend of a friend, or you receive an interview opportunity because of a loose connection that you and the recruiter share.

This was exactly the case for Abby England, who talked about the importance of genuine curiosity in building relationships in Chapter 2. Abby was connected to a well-known CMO on a job opportunity when she first moved to Atlanta from Bentonville, Arkansas. While the position wasn't exactly the right fit, the two stayed in touch.

Abby met a local recruiter at one of her very first Atlanta networking events. Just weeks after moving to Atlanta the recruiter introduced Abby to Jennifer Davis, a powerhouse CMO for Central States Building Works. Though Abby and Jennifer hit it off immediately, the timing and location weren't right for the role Jennifer had available.

Rather than letting the connection fade, Abby made small efforts to stay on Jennifer's radar. She sent Jennifer a Bentonville guide, commented on her social media posts, and maintained occasional contact through light, friendly exchanges. Eight months later, Jennifer reached out again—this time with a role located right outside Atlanta. Abby now holds that role.

"It's proof that investing in relationships is like compounding interest. It builds, even when you're not looking," Abby shared.

Again, Abby's connections with Jennifer were hardly dramatic gestures. They were friendly exchanges so that each of them stayed on one another's radar. While people tend to make "networking" feel more complex and tedious than it is, those easy exchanges—whether it's social media, email, virtual calls, or in-person meetings—are the whole ballgame. It doesn't demand a grand strategy, but it does require intentionality.

"I don't overthink it," Abby said. "If someone comes to mind, I act. Either I text them right away or I throw it on my calendar. My calendar is basically a to-do list, so if I can't act in the moment, I schedule it."

"I keep it real, light, and often informal," she added. "Sometimes it's just: 'wellness check–how are you?' No reason needed. Connection doesn't require a paragraph. Sometimes a funny gif keeps the thread alive."

We can apply this same logic to connections whom we haven't contacted over a period of time. One of the biggest mistakes people make in networking is assuming that reaching out to someone they haven't spoken to in years will feel forced or unwelcome. Consider the situation yourself. How do you feel when a longtime friend reaches out after not hearing from them for a while? Is your first reaction a cynical one? *Well, it sure is nice to hear from you, Johnny Come Lately?* Or is it a more genuine, *Wow, we haven't talked in quite some time. It's great to hear from you!* Most of the time, people truly appreciate it when someone takes the time to reconnect. Keep this in mind the next time you feel a little ambivalent about reaching out.

With that in mind, here are some other natural opportunities to reach out to colleagues and friends whom you might not have spoken to recently, but are looking for a way to reconnect.

- **Career Changes:** If you or the other person is starting a new role, launching a business, or pivoting industries, it's an excellent reason to check in.

- **Shared Interests or Industry News:** If you come across an article, podcast, or conference relevant to someone's work or passion, sending it along with a brief note is an easy way to stay on their radar.

- **Holidays and Anniversaries:** Year-end greetings, birthday wishes, or work anniversaries can be a low-pressure way to reconnect.

- **Mutual Acquaintances:** If you meet someone who reminds you of a former colleague or friend, reaching out with, "I met someone who made me think of you—how have you been?" can be a great conversation starter.

- **Random Acts of Connection:** Sometimes, no reason is needed. A simple, "Hey, I was thinking about you today. Hope you're doing well!" can go a long way.

CREATING WIN-WIN RELATIONSHIPS

Sometimes it makes sense to reach out cold to people who might be good connections for you. To illustrate this idea, I asked my friend Jo Ann Herold, who is the VP of Marketing & Public Relations for Georgia State University. Jo Ann intentionally read the local business paper, the *Atlanta Business Chronicle* to find a mentor. She was impressed by two people, but the first she reached out to was Hala Moddelmog, who is now the CEO of The Woodruff Arts Center, but was the president of Church's Chicken at the time. At that time, Jo Ann was the director of marketing for Honey Baked Ham. She asked Hala to lunch, and the two hit it off.

Jo Ann became her mentee, and also added value by helping Hala network with some private equity executives, leading to Hala becoming president of Arby's. Once Hala was there, she recruited Jo Ann to join her team. The reciprocity of the relationship has led to the mutual fulfillment and benefit for both Jo Ann and Hala.

Relationships like this don't just happen. They require intentionality and nurturing. "Hala will just pop into my head and I'll write her a handwritten note, just letting her know how grateful I am," Jo Ann said. "We'll connect for lunch. If I've got something that I think she'd be a great speaker for, she'll do that. So it's just staying connected and sharing gratitude."

Jo Ann went on to say: "I opened my own door initially, but these relationships have paid dividends thirty years later!"

When I asked Jo Ann how to really stand out, she reiterated a relic of the past that almost seems outdated today in an age of email, LinkedIn, Zoom, etc. "Handwritten notes. Nobody does that anymore," she said. These simple gestures convey a personal touch that digital media doesn't.

I recently hosted a dinner for Chief Marketing Officers of major companies at a Michelin-star restaurant with some of the best CMOs in Atlanta in attendance. We celebrated with some of the most superb food, drink, and service that the city has to offer. When I host a dinner like this, I try to begin by inviting the CMOs who are most influential so that we can get other marketing leaders to attend.

One of the first people that I invited was Jo Ann Herold, because I know she is an influencer. She made a special effort to attend the dinner, engage with all the other participants, and then talk up how amazing the dinner was afterwards. While Jo Ann was doing me a favor by attending, she followed up the event by sending me a beautiful, handwritten thank-you card. She included a personal note thanking me for including her with the "cool cats" of Atlanta marketing and for our decades of friendship.

It was a surprise to receive the card in the mail, since she was actually doing me a favor by attending. Of course, sending me that card further cements my fondness for Jo Ann and causes her to be top of mind as I think about opportunities that might be a good fit for her.

In addition to handwritten notes, Jo Ann is a believer in texting her relationships when she has downtime, for example,waiting for an appointment. Her outreach can be as simple as "I hope all is well. I am just thinking about you." It usually turns into a text thread that leads to an in-person coffee or lunch meeting.

A few additional tips from Jo Ann include sending gratitude cards to close connections at the beginning of each year and using LinkedIn to find people with common interests. This usually leads to coffee or a video call. One final tip that Jo Ann gave me related to LinkedIn was: "write somebody a LinkedIn recommendation, with no expectation that you're gonna get something back."

SMALL ACTIONS LEAD TO BIG IMPACT

Sustaining relationships doesn't require constant engagement, but it does require consistency.

A few small habits can make a significant difference in ensuring your connections remain strong:

- **Leverage Technology:** Use LinkedIn, email, or even texts to send short check-ins and updates.

- **Set Reminders:** If someone is particularly important to your network, set a reminder to check in every few months.

- **Share Your Wins and Celebrate Theirs:** Keeping people updated on what you're doing helps them stay engaged, and celebrating their successes deepens the relationship.

- **Make Introductions:** One of the best ways to maintain a connection is by helping someone else in their network. It keeps you top of mind and reinforces your role as a connector.

The most successful connectors operate with a mindset of generosity. This means offering value without expecting anything in return. Some ways to do this include:

- **Offer Help Before It's Asked For:** If you see someone struggling with a challenge you can solve, reach out with support.

- **Listen More Than You Talk:** People appreciate when they feel heard and understood. When you take the time to genuinely listen, you build deeper trust.

- **Give Without Expecting a Return:** The most authentic and meaningful relationships are those built on generosity. When you provide value—whether it's advice, an introduction, or encouragement—you naturally attract goodwill.

> **In the long run, maintaining relationships with a spirit of generosity leads to greater fulfillment and stronger connections. The relationships you invest in today will shape the opportunities you have tomorrow.**

Finally, building and maintaining long-term relationships isn't about keeping score. It's about fostering meaningful connections that last. Whether you are staying in touch with close friends, reconnecting with loose connections, or selflessly helping others, every relationship you nurture contributes to a thriving and supportive network. By approaching relationships with intentionality and generosity, you will not only enhance your career but also enrich your life in ways you never imagined.

FINDING YOUR TRUE NORTH

To give you a peek behind the curtain, during the writing of this book, I wrestled with whether to call this a "networking book." On the one hand, it would be broadly relatable and covers a topic on which most people understand they have to be proficient. At the same time, as we covered at the outset, "networking" can have such a negative connotation, because it conjures up images of standing in a crowded event space, talking to people with whom you don't really want to interact. Writing a "networking book" would mean constructing a how-to guide on improving in social situations that most people want to avoid altogether in the first place.

As a marketer, I can hardly think of a worse positioning strategy.

Indeed, if people think of networking only as a transactional exercise, going through the motions solely to gather names, emails, and LinkedIn profiles of individuals who might help you professionally further down the line, then of course it's going to feel burdensome.

Let's also be honest. We've all interacted with those overzealous networkers who say, "Let's connect on LinkedIn!" and then hand you their business card, before you've even had a chance to have a real conversation. These "networkers" approach the event as if they're a five-year-old collecting eggs at an Easter gathering, accumulating as many contacts as they can in an hour and a half. Of course, that approach to networking feels artificial. If your approach to networking is only to put your name out there, without any interest in learning about and helping others, "networking" will feel like an arduous chore, and you will likely be unsuccessful. It is specifically because of this misconception that "networking" gets such a bad rap in the first place.

Done well, networking is merely a tool that provides an opportunity to form a new relationship. **The relationship is the goal—not networking.** Human relationships are at the core of innovation, diverse teams, and building trust. If you think about your own personal growth and fulfillment, connection with other people will be at the heart of the process.

I was motivated to write this book specifically because people look at "networking" so narrowly.

Certainly, in some cases, networking involves talking to people you've never met in crowded event spaces. Some individuals, like me, enjoy these activities. Most, however, do not. There are so many better and healthier ways to build relationships with people, and my hope is that this book provides some helpful navigation tools for you.

In some cases, that may be asking thoughtful questions, either through an in-person conversation or on a video call. Curiosity spurs interest, and connections are forged over shared interests. In others, that could mean sharing details of your own challenge, or being attentive to the struggles someone else is going through. Or, it could involve listening to someone's problem, whether it's personal or professional, and responding with, "I think I know someone who might be able to help you."

If all of these situations sound like activities you already do, that is the point. All of those activities, which we explored in more detail in various chapters of this book, help form relationships. Too often, people seemingly make networking seem more tedious than it is. If you consciously adopt even a few of these exercises and practice them genuinely, your number of connections will grow, which will serve you well the next time you're looking to make a career move, your company is hiring, or if you're simply looking for recommendations on a yoga class.

Even more importantly, if you practice demonstrating curiosity, embracing vulnerability, or making meaningful introductions, the strength of these connections will also build up over time. By now, it should be abundantly clear that it's not about the sheer volume of names in your personal Rolodex, but rather on your level of trust, mentoring, and connection with these individuals.

More than furthering any professional end, building human relationships is ultimately about fulfillment. If you were to look back on the important milestones of your life—graduation, first job, marriage, work anniversary, etc.—those moments were special because of the people there with you. Relatedly, any type of achievement, whether it is earning a degree, garnering a promotion, or completing a marathon, happens because of the teachers, colleagues, and coaches around us.

To put it another way, human relationships determine our own happiness and, in some cases, our own survival. As the famous psychotherapist, Esther Perel says, 'The quality of your relationships determines the quality of your life."

In my case, relationships have helped me through every stage of life, whether that's through the joys of parenthood and growing my business, as well as the difficult moments. In turn, the connections that I have facilitated for others have led to job promotions, new startups, business acquisitions, and even a few marriages. Like so many stories in this book, relationships have led to wonderful personal and professional achievements, and they've also sustained me through life's most challenging events. These relationships, which I'm so proud of, were made possible through my network.

> **The skills in this book like curiosity, creativity, vulnerability, and diplomacy serve as your compass points, helping you navigate toward deeper, more meaningful connections. When you orient yourself toward genuine interest in others rather than transactional networking, you find your true north: the understanding that authentic relationships are both the journey and the destination.**

Continue to build the most meaningful relationships that you can. In the end, they are the only thing that matters.

END NOTES

1. Marissa King, *Social Chemistry: Decoding the Patterns of Human Connection* (New York: Dutton, 2022).

2. Gino Wickman and Mark C. Winters, *Rocket Fuel: The One Essential Combination That Will Get You More of What You Want from Your Business* (Dallas: BenBella Books, 2015).

3. David Nour, *Relationship Economics: Transform Your Most Valuable Business Contacts into Personal and Professional Success*, 3rd ed. (Hoboken, NJ: Wiley, 2019).

4. Napoleon Hill, *Think and Grow Rich* (Meriden, CT: The Ralston Society, 1937), chap. 10 ("The Power of the Master Mind"). For the quoted line ("No two minds ever come together..."), see "Think and Grow Rich: Chapter 10. Power of the Master Mind," Sacred-Texts, accessed October 14, 2025, https://www.sacred-texts.com/nth/tgr/tgr15.htm.

5. Centers for Disease Control and Prevention, "Data and Statistics on ADHD," updated November 19, 2024, accessed October 14, 2025, https://www.cdc.gov/adhd/data/index.html.

6. Bright Pink. "About Us." https://www.brightpink.org/about-us-1. Accessed November 20, 2025.

7. Alex Kerai, "Cell Phone Usage Statistics 2023: Mornings Are for Notifications," *Reviews.org*, May 9, 2023, accessed October 14, 2025,https://www.reviews.org/mobile/2023-cell-phone-addiction/.

8. Jennifer Dorian (President & CEO, WABE), interview by author, 2025.

9. Abby England (Head of Marketing., Elevate Structures), interview by author, 2025.

10. Tim Hernquist (Head of Enterprise Marketing, Jabra), interview by author, 2025.

11. Melissa M. Proctor (EVP & Chief Marketing Officer, Atlanta Hawks / State Farm Arena), interview by author, 2025.

12. Stacey Tank (Chief Executive Officer, Bespoke Beauty Brands), interview by author, 2025.

13. Darrah Brustein (Executive Coach; Contributing Writer, Inc. Magazine), interview by author, 2025.

14. Jason Dominy (Marketing Strategist, Flat Six Consulting), interview by author, 2025.

15. Moira Vetter (Founder & CEO, Modo Modo Agency), interview by author, 2025.

16. Adam Albrecht (Founder & CEO, The Weaponry), interview by author, 2025.

17. Amanda M. Thompson (President, Setup), interview by author, 2025.

ACKNOWLEDGMENTS

Family and Friends

To **Joss and Radley**—my true north. You reminded me daily that connection is the point, not the prize.

To my immediate family—**my mom, Lois; her partner, Robert; my brother, Clif,** and **my beloved, Lynn**—thank you for patience, cheerleading, and the reality checks that helped me finish.

To my extended family both by blood and choice. Thank you. You have shaped me in ways I could not even imagine.

Jeff Hilimire—for model-by-doing leadership and the generous pushes to ship.

Rachelle Kuramoto—I could not have asked for a better foreword writer or friend.

The other Ripples Media authors—for community, candor, and momentum when the pages felt heavy.

The Setup Journey

To the Setup **team—past and present**—thank you for turning a passion for matchmaking into disciplined practice. Every intake, brief, and introduction sharpened the ideas in these pages.

Current team: Amanda M. Thompson, Rho Beckmann, Madeline Evans, May Amor Beja, Kayla Floyd, Meghan Hilton.

Past team: Stephanie Peterman, Katia Herrera, Anastasia Kusmarteseva Fussell, William Denning, Kate Jacoutot, Sam Moran, Ethan Parrish, Tiffany Ujjin, Zevi Solomon, Alexis Quarcoo, Evan Rosenthal.

To early colleagues who shaped my craft at prior stops—thank you for the reps and rigor that prepared me for Setup.

Voices Featured in the Book

Thank you to the leaders who shared their stories and thinking—your words lifted these pages: **Jennifer Dorian** (WABE); **Abby England** (Elevate Structures); **Tim Hernquist** (Jabra); **Melissa M. Proctor** (Atlanta Hawks/State Farm Arena); **Jason Dominy** (Flat Six Consulting); **Moira Vetter** (Modo Modo Agency); **Adam Albrecht** (The Weaponry); **Stacey Tank** (Bespoke Beauty Brands); **Amanda M. Thompson** (Setup).

Communities & Classrooms

To **AMA Atlanta, Fuse (formerly AIMA),** and **UGA's Terry College of Business** (including Jen Osbon)— thank you for the community you provide including the platforms, panels, and students who challenged my thinking and sharpened the craft.

To **Everybody Wins! Atlanta**—reading with students each week kept me grounded in the simple act of attention.

Publishing & Production

To **Ripples Media**—for believing in this project and helping turn lived practice into a usable book. Special thanks to **Andrew Vogel, Nicole Wedekind,** and **Dorothy Miller-Farleo (DMF)** for the steady guidance and care.

To the editors, designers, and proofreaders behind the scenes—thank you for pace, clarity, and a clean, modern compass.

To my early readers: **Rachelle Kuramoto, Todd Slutzky, Amanda M. Thompson,** and **Robert Jolly**—I cannot thank you enough for your time and attention to detail helping me get this book to the finish line. I truly could not have done it without you.

My Street Team

To the clients, peers, and friends who marked up early drafts, pushed on soft spots, and asked for clearer playbooks—your tough love made this a field guide, not a memoir.

A Final Thank You

To everyone who has ever asked, "Who should I meet?"—and then said yes to an introduction—this book is for you. One thoughtful connection can change everything.

ABOUT THE AUTHOR

Joe Koufman is a lifelong connector of people and ideas. In 2014 he founded Setup, a firm that helps marketers level up by matching brands with the right agencies and resources—facilitating 1,200+ introductions in its first decade. Previously, Joe served as SVP of Marketing & Business Development at Engauge (acquired by Publicis Groupe in 2013) and led strategic accounts at KnowledgeStorm (acquired by TechTarget in 2007).

Beyond the office, Joe is fueled by music, art, and culture. For many years, he hosted a weekly music show at GumboShow.com, and he is learning to play a 100-year-old trumpet he inherited from his grandmother. Joe has served his community through his board tenure with AMA Atlanta, Fuse (formerly AIMA), and the Terry College of Business at the University of Georgia, and he volunteers with Everybody Wins! Atlanta. A graduate of Wake Forest University in Speech Communication and Politics, he jokes he uses the former daily—and the latter more often than he'd like.

Joe lives in Atlanta and spends weekends exploring concerts, galleries, and the outdoors with his twins, Joss and Radley. The Connector's Compass is his first book.

ABOUT RIPPLES MEDIA

RIPPLES MEDIA is a community-driven publisher working with business leaders and socially conscious changemakers to tell stories that matter. Our purpose is simple: to fill the world with authentic stories that inspire positive change.

We believe the right story, told well, can spark understanding and create ripples of impact in communities and in business. Each book we publish becomes part of a growing movement of leaders using their voices to make a difference.

LEARN MORE AT RIPPLES.MEDIA